EDITION 38 2016
Copyright ©
Geographers' A-Z Map Company Ltd.
Telephone: 01732 781000 (Enquiries & Trade Sales)
          01732 783422 (Retail Sales)

The representation on the maps of any other road,
track or footpath is no evidence of the existence of
a right of way.

Note 1. Each place name is followed by the reference to its map position; e.g. **Admiralty** Whitehall is to be found in square 4A on page 82. (Places preceded by an *asterisk are outside Central London area mapped.)

Note 2. Each station name is followed by the reference/s (abbreviated) to the Underground Line/s (or outside the Underground network the Main Line Railway Station) serving it. For example, Goodge Street N. means that station is on the Underground Northern Line.

Abbreviations are: B=Bakerloo; Cen.=Central; Cir.=Circle; D.=District; DLR.=Docklands Light Railway; H.=Hammersmith & City; J.=Jubilee; M.=Metropolitan; N.=Northern; O.=Overground; P.=Piccadilly; V. =Victoria.

For central area Underground Map, see back cover.

RECOMMENDED SIGHTSEEING

- ❁❁❁ Places not to be missed
- ❁❁ Highly recommended
- ❁ Recommended
- ❁ Recommended for families with children

■ ***ACCESS FOR THE DISABLED***
Artsline and Inclusive London online disability access information services, can provide up-to-date advice and access details to London's Museums, Galleries, Cinemas, Theatres, Concert Halls and other tourist attractions.
www.artsline.org.uk
www.inclusivelondon.com

■ ***Abbey Road Recording Studios,** NW1, off Grove End Road / Circus Road. 3A 58 ❁
The world famous recording studios and nearby that iconic 'Beatles Album' zebra crossing. *Station:* St. John's Wood. J

■ **Admiralty & Admiralty Arch,** Whitehall. 4A 82
Once the administrative and operational centre of the British Navy. The Old Admiralty building dates from 1722 a handsome screen by Adam being added c.1760.
The large triple archway of Admiralty Arch opens on to the Mall and the quiet of St. James's Park. State and Royal processions pass through it on their way between Buckingham Palace and Westminster Abbey and/or the Houses of Parliament. *Station:* Charing Cross. B.N.

■ **Albert Memorial,** Kensington Gardens. 1E 89 ❁
Designed by Sir Gilbert Scott, it was erected as a memorial to Prince Albert, Consort of Queen Victoria, at a cost of £120,000, and took 20 years to construct.

Station: South Kensington. Cir.D.P.

■ **Alexander Fleming Museum,** St Mary's Hospital, Praed Street. 4A 66 The laboratory in which Fleming discovered penicillin, displays and video presentation. Admission charge. Open: 10 a.m. to 1 p.m. Mon. to Thurs. other times by appointment. *Station:* Paddington. B.Cir.D.H

■ **Apsley House,** Hyde Park Corner. 5A 80 ✪
This Adam's building was bought by the famous Duke of Wellington as his London House. It is now the Wellington Museum and contains trophies of the Napoleonic Wars, uniforms, swords and decorations. *Admission Charge.* Open: Wednesday to Sunday 11 a.m. to 5 p.m. Summer. Saturday and Sunday 10 a.m. to 4 p.m. Winter. Closed Christmas and New Year *Station:* Hyde Park Corner. P.

■ **Bank of England,** Threadneedle Street. 5F 73
Known as the 'Old Lady of Threadneedle Street' this is the Governments Bank, incorporated under Royal Charter in 1694 to find for the Government £1,200,000 required for the war against France's Louis XIV. Only the massive external wall survives of Sir John Soanes' design of 1833. *Station:* Bank. Cen. DLR. N.

■ **Bank of England Museum,** Bartholomew Lane. 4F 73
The history of the Bank of England from its foundation in 1694 to its role today as the nation's central bank. Displays include banknotes, coins, gold bullion, interactive videos and a reconstructed 18th century banking hall.
Open: Mon. to Fri. 10 a.m. to 5 p.m. Closed Sat. Sun. and Public Holidays. *Station:* Bank. Cen. DLR. N.

■ **Bankside Gallery,** Hopton Street. 2C 84
Gallery of the Royal Watercolour Society and Royal Society of Painter-Printmakers. Open during exhibitions daily 11 a.m. to 6 p.m. *Stations:* Blackfriars. Cir.D. Southwark. J.

■ **Banqueting House,** Whitehall 4B 82 ✪✪
Commissioned by James I, and built by Inigo Jones it was completed in 1622; and embellished by Charles I, with the famous painted ceiling by Rubens. The artist was rewarded with £3,000 and a knighthood. It was through a window of the Banqueting House that King Charles went to his execution in 1649. It is the only surviving building of Whitehall Palace. *Admission Charge.* Open daily 10 a.m. to 1 p.m; to 5 p.m. when not in use for functions, to check telephone 020 3166 6155. Closed Christmas and New Year. *Stations:* Charing Cross. B.N. Westminster. Cir.D.J.

■ **Barbican.** 2E 73 ✪ A large area of post-war redevelopment designed to reintroduce a balanced residential and cultural life back into the heart of the business City. Pedestrians are segregated from traffic on elevated levels, and accommodation is grouped around squares, gardens and lakes. The historic church of St. Giles and a length of the Roman and Medieval City Wall are incorporated. The precinct includes the following: Barbican Arts Centre, Museum of London, Guildhall School of Music and Drama, City of London School for Girls.

Opened in 1982 the **Barbican Arts Centre** facilities include: Barbican Hall, Barbican Theatre, Barbican Library, Art Gallery, Cinemas, conference and trade exhibition space and roof-top Conservatory. Foyer open daily with exhibitions, bookshop and restaurants. Car park. *Stations:* Barbican. Cir.M.H. Moorgate. Cir.M.H.

■ **BBC Broadcasting House,** Portland Place. 3C 68
This famous landmark art deco building was completed in 1932, It houses the headquarters, sound division and new state-of-the-art multimedia centre of the British Broadcasting Corporation. *Station:* Oxford Circus. B.Cen.V.

■ **Belfast H.M.S.,** Morgan's Lane. 3C 86 ✪ ✪
This 10,500 ton cruiser, launched in 1938, the last major warship of the 1939-45 war still afloat, is now a naval museum and part of the Imperial War Museum.
Admission Charge. Open: Summer 10 a.m. to 6 p.m., Winter 10 a.m. to 5 p.m. Closed Christmas Eve and Day, Boxing Day. *Station:* London Bridge. J.N.

■ **Benjamin Franklin House,** 36 Craven Street. 3B 82
18th century home of the American scientist, philosopher, printer, writer, inventor, diplomat and Founding Father of the United States, restored to its original period condition.
Admission Charge. Open for Historical Experience shows 12 a.m. to 4.15 p.m. Wed. to Sun. Architectural tours on Mondays. Pre book 020 7925 1405. *Stations:* Charing Cross. B.N. Embankment. Cir.D.

■ **Big Ben.** Westminster. 1C 94 ✪✪✪
Although popularly used to describe the clock tower, Big Ben is in fact the name of the 13$\frac{1}{2}$ ton bell which strikes the hours. It was cast at the Whitechapel Foundry in 1858. The 320 foot tower was renamed Elizabeth Tower in 2012 to honour the Queen's Diamond Jubilee.
Station: Westminster. Cir.D.J.

■ **Billingsgate,** Lower Thames Street. 2B 86
The name of London's oldest market, it was restricted in the 17th century to dealing in fish. The 1874 Market Hall facade is incorporated into the redeveloped site following the removal of trading to the Isle of Dogs in 1982.
Stations: Monument. Cir.D. Tower Hill. Cir.D.

■ **Bond Street.** 1C 80 The upper end which runs into Oxford Street is New Bond Street, and the lower end which runs into Piccadilly is Old Bond Street. This expensive

4

London shopping street ranks in world fame with the Rue
de la Paix in Paris, and New York's Fifth Avenue.
Stations: Bond Street. Cen.J. Green Park. J.P.V.

■ **Borough Market,** Bedale Street. 4F 85   This important
wholesale market has, since 1998, been supplemented by
an ever growing, popular, award winning fine food retail
market crammed with both Londoner and tourist foodies
alike.   Open Wed and Thurs 10 a.m. to 5 p.m. Fri to 6 pm.
& Sat 8 a.m. to 5 p.m. *Station*: London Bridge. J.N.

■ **BFI Southbank,** Southbank. 3E 83   British Film Institute
venue for creative, archive and themed film seasons. Bars,
restaurants, shop. BFI Library has an extensive collection
of books, periodicals and historic archive materials. Open
daily. *Stations*: Embankment. B.Cir.D. Waterloo. B.J.N.

■ **British Library,** Euston Road. 3A 62 ✪✪✪
The worlds leading resource for scholarship and research,
its new climate controlled building has 11 reading rooms,
seating for 1200 researchers and nearly 14 million volumes
stored in 4 levels of basements.   The public exhibition
rooms include The Treasures Gallery housing some 200 of
the most famous items including Lindisfarne Gospels,
Magna Carta, Anglo-Saxon Chronicle, Gutenburg Bible,
Shakespeare's First Folio, Nelson's log books, Scott's
Antarctic Journal.
   Special exhibitions are mounted throughout the year.
Treasures Gallery and Public areas, cafe, bookshop: open
Mon and Fri: 9.30 a.m. to 6 p.m. Tues, Wed and Thurs to 8
p.m. Sat. to 5 p.m. Sun. 11 a.m. to 5 p.m.
Reading Rooms: open to ticket holders only for research
only. Closed Christmas, and New Year.
*Station:*King's Cross St. Pancras. Cir.D.M.N.P.V.

■ **British Museum,** Great Russell Street. 3A 70 ✪✪✪ ✪
Originally founded in 1753 from several private collections
this rapidly became the finest Museum in existence. Its
unrivalled collections are comprised in the Departments of
Coins and Medals, Egyptian Antiquities, Western Asiatic
Antiquities, Greek and Roman Antiquities, (including the
famous Elgin Marbles), British and Medieval Antiquities
Oriental Antiquities and Prints and Drawings
   The famous former Reading Room is now the centrepiece
of the restored inner courtyard, a spectacular covered
public square 'The Great Court' with restaurants, museum
shops, education facilities; giving access both through the
museum and between the surrounding galleries.
   Special exhibitions are mounted throughout the year.
Open: 10 a.m. to 5.30 p.m. daily and extended opening on
Fridays to 8.30 p.m. Closed Christmas the New Year Day.
Free lectures on certain days.
Stations: Russell Square. P. Tottenham Court Road. C.N.

■ **Brompton Oratory, The,** Brompton Road. 3B 90 ✪
Built in the Italian Renaissance style during the 19th century, it is well known for its fine musical services. Cardinal Newman served here as priest after his conversion from the Anglican to the Roman Catholic faith. Open: 6 a.m. to 8 p.m. *Station:* South Kensington. Cir.D.P.

■ **Buckingham Palace,** The Mall, 1C 92 ✪✪✪
London Palace of Her Majesty Queen Elizabeth II. When she is in residence the Royal Standard flies from the mast, at other times the Union Flag is flown. Changing of the Guard takes place daily at 11.30 a.m. on certain days, see *Pageantry* for details. Built by the Duke of Buckingham in 1703. Buckingham Palace was bought by George III in 1761, was rebuilt again by George IV, and became Queen Victoria's London home. Refaced in 1913. The Queen's Gallery, which forms part of the private chapel destroyed in the Second World War, contains a varying exhibition of masterpieces and works of art from the royal art treasures.
STATE ROOMS Open: During August and September by timed ticket only. Day tickets from Visitor Entrance ticket office. For details and advanced tickets Tel: 020 7766 7300 / 7301 or 7302. Admission Charge.
QUEEN'S GALLERY Open (except during changes of exhibition) 10 to 5.30pm daily. Admission by timed ticket, Tel: 020 7766 7301 for advance tickets. Admission charge.
ROYAL MEWS Open: 1 April - 31 October daily. Monday to Saturday at other times. Closed December and on specific days and State Visits; details and advanced tickets on Tel: 020 7766 7302 Admission Charge.
Stations: Green Park. J.P.V. St. James's Park. Cir.D. Victoria. Cir.D.V.

■ ***Camden Lock Market,** Camden High Street, off Parkway 1B 60   A popular lively street market on Sat. and Sun. in an interesting canalside setting; clothes, crafts, antiques etc. *Station:* Camden Town. N.

■ ***Camden Passage,** N1   *Station:* Angel N.
A popular centre for antique arcades and shops. *Station:* Angel. N.

■ ***Carlyle's House,** 24 Cheyne Row, SW3
The famous writer lived here from 1834 until his death in 1881. The house has hardly been altered since. Now a National Trust property. *Admission Charge.* Open: April to October 11 a.m. to 4.30 p.m. Wednesday to Sunday. *Station:* Sloane Square. Cir.D.

■ **Carnaby Street.** 5D 69
Popular teenage fashion centre of the late 1960's. *Stations:* Oxford Circus. B. Cen. V. Piccadilly Circus. B.P.

■ **Cartoon Museum,** 35 Little Russell Street, 3B 70
See the finest examples of British cartoons, caricature and comic art from the 18th century to the present day. Resource centre and shop. *Admission Charge.*
Open: 10.30am to 5.30pm Mon. to Sat. 12 a.m. to 5.30 p.m. Sunday. *Station:* Tottenham Court Road. Cen. N.

■ **Cenotaph, The,** Whitehall. 5B 82
Designed by Sir Edwin Lutyens, it now stands as a perpetual memorial to 'The Glorious Dead' of both World Wars. On the Sunday nearest November 11th of each year, crowds gather at the Cenotaph for the two minutes silence, and wreaths are laid by the Queen, members of the Government and other mourners.
Stations: Charing Cross. B.N. Westminster. Cir.D.J.

■ **Central Criminal Court,** Old Bailey. 4B 72
Known as 'The Old Bailey', the present building was completed in 1907 on the site of Newgate Prison. The lofty tower is surmounted by a bronze gilt figure of Justice. During important trials in Court 1, a large crowd gathers outside in the hope of gaining admission to the Public Gallery in Newgate Street, which seats 28. Five other courts seat up to 32 each. Open: Monday to Friday 9.55 a.m. to 12.40 p.m. and 1.55 p.m. to 3.40 p.m. No children under 14 admitted. *Station:* St. Paul's. Cen.

■ **Central Hall,** Tothill Street 1A 94
This large domed building is the Methodists' London Headquarters. It is often used for conferences, exhibitions and concerts. The first session of the General Assembly of the United Nations took place here in 1946.
Stations: Westminster. Cir.D.J. St. James's Park. Cir.D.

■ **Charles Dickens Museum** 48 Doughty Street. 1E 71
Although the author lived here only from 1837 to 1839, 'Oliver Twist' and 'Nicholas Nickelby' were written and the 'Pickwick Papers' completed during those two years. The house is now a Museum of Dickens Memorabilia, and the headquarters of the Dickens Fellowship.
Admission Charge. Open: 10 a.m. to 5 p.m. daily. Closed Christmas and New Year. *Station:* Russell Square. P.

■ ***Chelsea Physic Garden,** 66 Royal Hospital Road, off Lower Sloane Street. SW3 5F 91.
Botanic gardens established in 1673 for the propagation and study of new species, from which several staple industries in former British colonies were derived.
Admission Charge. Open: April to October: Tuesday to Friday, also Sunday and Bank Holidays 11 a.m. to 6 p.m. November to March: 9.30 a.m. to 4 p.m. or dusk Monday to Friday. Entrance in Swan Walk, SW3.
Station: Sloane Square. Cir.D.

■ **Cheshire Cheese,** Ye Olde. Wine Office Court, 145 Fleet Street. 4A 72
An old and little-altered inn featuring numerous small, darkly atmospheric panelled rooms. Tradition has it that Dr. Johnson Boswell, Oliver Goldsmith and Dickens were habitues. Built in 1667 over cellars dating back to 1538.
Open: Bar daily Mon. to Sat. Restaurant Lunch daily, Dinner Mon. to Sat. *Station:* Blackfriars. Cir.D.

■ **Chinatown.** 1A 82
A lively centre of oriental sights, sounds and aromas, complete with chinese style gateways and telephone boxes. Between Shaftesbury Avenue and Leicester Square. *Station:* Leicester Square. N. P.

■ **Christie's,** 8 King Street. 3E 81
Founded in 1766, greatly reputed for its auction sales of valuable paintings furniture, silver, jewels, etc. held regularly. Telephone 020 7839 9060 for details.
Station: Green Park. J.P.V.

■ **Churchill War Rooms,** King Charles Street. 5A 82 ✪✪
Used by Winston Churchill and his staff during World War II. Visit the cabinet room, central map room, Churchill's office and bedroom, the dining room, the transatlantic telephone room etc,. all restored to their wartime appearance. The Churchill Museum illustrates his life, work and achievements. *Admission charge.* Open 9.30 a.m. to 6 p.m. daily. Closed 24, 25 and 26 December.
Station: Westminster. Cir.D.J.

■ **Cinema Museum,** Dugard Way. SE11. 4B 96
Covering all aspects of cinema history and cinema going. *Admission charge.* Open: Pre Booked tours only, Tel: 020 7840 2200. *Station:* Elephant & Castle B. N..

■ **City Hall,** Tooley Street. 4C 86
The unique spherical glass-walled headquarters of the Greater London Authority. Public access to landscaped piazzas and internal spiral ramp to the 10th floor viewing gallery with panoromic views. *Station:* London Bridge. J.N.

■ **Clarence House,** St. James's Palace. 5E 81 ✪✪
Built in the 1840's to designs by John Nash for the Duke of Clarence. A Royal residence for over 170 years but known primarily as the home of Queen Elizabeth the Queen Mother who lived here 1953-2002. Now official residence of the Prince of Wales. Admission charge. Open: August 10 a.m. to 4.30 p.m. Monday to Friday; to 5.30 p.m. Saturday and Sunday. Admission by timed ticket only. 020 7766 7303   *Station:* Green Park. J.P.V.

■ **Cleopatra's Needle,** Victoria Embankment. 3D 83 ✪
An Egyptian obelisk which, about 3,500 years ago, stood

in front of the Temple of the Sun at Heliopolis. When it was being towed to England in 1877, this 'Needle', 68½ feet high and weighing 180 tons, had to be abandoned in the Bay of Biscay during a storm. Its sister column is sited in Central Park, New York. *Station:* Embankment. B.Cir.D.N.

■ **Clink Prison Museum,** Clink Street. 3F 85
Illustrates the history of the prison and the infamous low life of this area, once known as 'The Liberty of the Clink'. Admission Charge. Open: Summer daily 10am to 9pm. Winter to 6 pm. Mon. to Fri., to 7.30 pm. Sat. and Sun. *Station:* London Bridge. J.N.

■ **College of Arms,** or Heralds College, Queen Victoria Street. 1D 85   Deals with all matters relating to Heraldry genealogy and State Ceremonials and consists of three Kings of Arms (Garter, Clarenceux, and Norroy & Ulster), six Heralds and four Pursuivants, appointed by the Sovereign. The building, Derby House, reconstructed after the Great Fire, was presented to the College by Queen Mary I (Mary Tudor) in 1555.   The panelled Earl Marshal's Court is open 10 a.m. to 4 p.m. Mon. to Fri. (also open for heraldic enquiries). Closed public holidays.
Stations: Blackfriars. Cir.D. Mansion House. Cir. D.

■ **Courtauld Gallery,** Somerset House. 1D 83 ✪✪
Contains a famous collection of Impressionist and Post-Impressionist masterpieces by Matisse, Derain, Manet, Renoir, Van Gogh and Cezanne, and important works from the Renaissance through to the 20th century. Part of the Courtauld Institute of Art. See also Somerset House.
Admission Charge. Daily 10 a.m. to 6 p.m. Closed Christmas. Stations: Temple. Cir.D. Charing Cross. N.B.

■ **Covent Garden,** Southampton Street, WC2 1C 82 ✪✪✪
Originally 'Convent Garden' the square is now pedestrianised with the central market hall restored and open as an environment of shops, studios, cafes; promenades and paved areas are venues for lively street theatre. The Flower Market now houses the London Transport Museum.
Given a Royal Charter in 1671, the market grew into London's largest wholesale fruit, vegetable and flower market. Moved 1974 to a new site off Nine Elms Lane SW8.
Stations: Covent Garden. P. Leicester Square. N. P.

■ **Contemporary Applied Arts,** 89 Southwark Street, 4C 84
Changing exhibitions of work by artist-craftsmen.
Open 10 a.m. to 6 p.m. Mon. to Sat. *Station:* Southwark. J.

■ **Custom House,** Lower Thames Street. 2B 86
Until 1940, the headquarters of the Commissioners of Customs and Excise, this has been the approximate site of successive Custom Houses from the 14th century. The

impressive riverside facade is by Robert Smirke c.1825.
Stations: Monument. Cir.D. Tower Hill. Cir.D.

■ **Cutty Sark,** see Outer London. 🟢🟢🟢 🟢

■ **Dennis Severs' House,** 18 Folgate Street. 2C 74
18th century house and experience, illustrates the lives of
the Huguenot silk-weavers who once lived here.
Admission Charge. Open:12 - 4 p.m. Sunday. 12 - 2 p.m.
Monday. Book for themed tours at other times 020 7247
4013. *Station:* Liverpool Street Cen.Cir.H.M.

■ **Design Museum,** Shad Thames. 4E 87 (Until late 2016)
Covers the history, practice, theory and future of design in
mass-produced consumer products and services.
Admission Charge. Open: 10 a.m. to 5.15 p.m. daily.
Stations: London Bridge. J.N. Tower Hill. Cir.D.
Note: Moves late 2016 to Kensington High Street off 2A 88

■ **Diana, Princess of Wales Memorial Fountain,** Hyde
Park. 5A 78 Memorial to the late Princess who died 1997.
Stations: Knightsbridge. P. Lancaster Gate. C.

■ **Doctor Johnson's House,** 17 Gough Square. 4A 72
The famous 18th-century writer immortalised by Boswell,
lived here from 1748 to 1759. The house contains an early
edition of his Dictionary which was compiled here and
published in 1755 selling for four guineas. Here also he
wrote 'The Rambler' which appeared twice weekly for two
years with a circulation of about five hundred.
Admission Charge. Open: 11 a.m. to 5.30 p.m. (Winter 5
p.m.) Closed Sundays and Bank Holidays.
Station: Chancery Lane. Cen.

■ **Downing Street,** Whitehall. 5B 82 🟢
No.10 Downing Street is world-famous as the home of the
British Prime Minister and the scene of Cabinet meetings.
No. 11 houses the Chancellor of the Exchequer, and No.
12 is the Government Whip's office.
Station: Westminster. Cir.D.J.

■ **Duke of York's Column,** Waterloo Place. 4F 81 🟢
This column, which stands above the steps leading to St.
James's Park, is 124 feet high, and was erected in 1833 as
a memorial to Frederick, Duke of York, the second son of
George III. Although an able and devoted Army
administrator, as Commander-in-Chief he was less
successful in the field: according to popular song he 'led
his ten thousand men up a hill and then he led them down
again'! *Stations:* Piccadilly Circus. B.P. Charing Cross. B.N

■ **Embankment Galleries,** Somerset House. 1E 83
Venue for themed exhibitions. See also **Somerset House**.
Admission Charge. Open: 10 a.m. to 6 p.m.

■ **Eros,** see Piccadilly Circus. 🟢🟢🟢

■ **Faraday Museum** see Royal Institution Museum.

■ **Fashion & Textile Museum,** 83 Bermondsey Street.
5C 86 The first museum in the UK devoted to
contemporary fashion and textiles. *Admission Charge.*
Open Tuesday to Saturday 11 a.m. to 6 p.m; to 8 p.m.
Thursday. 11 to 5 p.m. Sunday during exhibitions.
Station: London Bridge. J. N.

■ **Florence Nightingale Museum,** Lambeth Palace Road,
1D 95   Illustrates the life and work of this famous woman,
including a life size reconstruction of a ward at the Crimea.
Admission Charge. Open: 10 a.m. to 5 p.m. daily. Closed
Christmas and Easter.
Stations: Westminster. Cir.D.J. Waterloo. B.J.N.

■ **Foundling Museum,** 40 Bruswick Square. 5C 62
Interiors from the former Foundling Hospital, founded 1739
for the care of destitute children. Displays include pictures
donated by Hogarth, Gainsborough, Knellar, also Handel's
own copy of the 'Messiah'.
Admission Charge. Open 10 a.m. to 5 p.m. Tues. to Sat.,
11 to 5 p.m. Sunday. Closed Christmas and New Year.
Station: Russell Square. P.

■ **Garden Museum,** Lambeth Palace Road. 3D 95.
Permanant and temporary displays exploring themes on
garden history, including chronology, tools and plant
hunters - like the Tradescants - gardeners to Charles I,
responsible for introducing many exotic plants into
England; also related art exhibitions.
Admission charge. Open: 10.30 a.m. to 5 p.m. Sunday to
Friday; to 4 p.m. Saturday. Closed first Monday of every
month. *Station:* Westminster. Cir.D.J.

■ ***Geffrye Museum,** Kingsland Road, E2.
Housed in Almshouses erected in 1915 by the
Ironmongers' Company. It comprises a series of period
rooms dating from the 16th to the 20th century, containing
furniture, domestic equipment and musical instruments
from middle class homes. Open: 10 a.m. to 5 p.m. Sun.
12 to 5 p.m. Closed Mon. (except Bank Holiday Mondays)
also Christmas and New Year. *Station:* Old Street. N.

■ **Globe Theatre,** see Shakespeare's Globe Theatre.

■ **Golden Hinde,** St Mary Overie Dock, Cathedral Street.
3F 85 ✪ Floating museum ship, a full scale, ocean-going
reconstruction of Sir Francis Drake's famous galleon.
Admission Charge. Open: Daily 10 a.m to 5.30 p.m. unless
closed for functions. *Station:* London Bridge. J.N.

■ **Goldsmiths' Hall,** Foster Lane. 4D 73
Home of the Goldsmiths' Company, one of the twelve
Great Livery Companies of the City of London. Since 1281
a jury containing several goldsmiths has been responsible

11

for the Trial of the Pyx, the testing of newly minted coins, and from 1870 this has been held annually at Goldsmiths Hall. Gold and silver are assayed and hallmarked here.
Station: St. Paul's. Cen.

■ **Grant Museum of Zoology,** 21 University Street, 1F 69
Founded in 1828 as a teaching collection, its displays cover the whole Animal Kingdom, including many species now endangered or extinct.
Open 1 to 5 p.m. Mon. to Sat. Closed Christmas and Easter. *Station:* Euston Square. Cir.D.H.

■ **Gray's Inn,** High Holborn. 2E 71 ❂
One of the four great Inns of Court. The historic Elizabethan Hall has been fully restored since the war. The Chapel also suffered damage by bombing. Francis Bacon, who was a student of the Inn, is said to have planted the catalpa tree in the gardens.
Station: Chancery Lane. Cen. Holborn. Cen. P.

■ **Green Park.** 4C 80 ❂
Covers an area of 53 acres. The fine iron gateway on the Piccadilly side is that of old Devonshire House.
Stations: Green Park. J.P.V. Hyde Park Corner. P.

■ **Greenwich,** see Outer London. ❂❂❂ ❂

■ **Guard's Chapel,** see Guards Museum.

■ **Guards Museum,** Birdcage Walk. 1E 93
Illustrates the 300-year history of the Brigade of Guards comprising five regiments of Her Majesties Foot Guards - the Grenadier, Coldstream, Scots, Irish and Welsh Guards. Adjacent is Guard's Chapel, rebuilt 1963 following destruction by a flying bomb in 1944.
Admission Charge. Open 10 a.m. to 4 p.m. daily. Closed Christmas. *Station:* St James's Park. Cir.D.

■ **Guildhall,** Gresham Street. 4F 73 ❂
The centre of civic government in the City of London for more than a thousand years. Dating from 1411-39 the structure of the present Hall survived both the Great Fire of 1666, and World War II bombs, though the only original interior is the fine medieval fan vaulted crypt.
The Great Hall is used for the Presentation of the Freedom of the City and other civic functions. Here the Livery Companies, twelve of whose banners hang from the walls, annually elect the new Lord Mayor and Sheriffs. The Lord Mayor's procession is held on the second Saturday in November and the banquet the following Monday.
Modern extensions contains the **Guildhall Library,** a major public reference library specialising in the history of London, especially the City. The **Guildhall Art Gallery** features both the collection of the Corporation of London - particularly rich in Victorian Art and the dramatically

presented remains of the **Roman Ampitheatre** preserved within the building.
Open: Guildhall (Subject to functions), 10 a.m. to 4.30 p.m. daily, closed winter Sundays.
Library 9.30 a.m. to 5 p.m. Mon. to Fri. to 7.30 p.m. Wed. Gallery and Ampitheatre 10 a.m. to 5 p.m. Mon. to Sat. 12.00 to 4 p.m. Sun. *Station:* Bank. Cen. DLR. N.

■ **Hampton Court Palace,** see Outer London ✪✪✪

■ **Handel House Museum,** 25 Brook Street. 1B 80
Handel's home from 1723 to his death 1759 and where he composed many famous works including Messiah and Music for the Royal Fireworks.
Admission charge. Open 10 a.m. to 6 p.m. Tues to Sat, to 8 p.m. Thurs. 12 to 6 p.m. Sun. Closed Mondays and Christmas. *Station:* Bond Street. Cen.J.

■ **Hatton Garden,** Holborn. 2A 72
Stands partly on the site of the old palace of the Bishop of Ely. It is well known as an important centre of the world's diamond trade. *Station:* Farringdon. Cir.H.M.

■ **Hayward Gallery,** Belvedere Road, South Bank. 4E 83 ✪
Changing shows of either modern art, a historical theme or international loan exhibitions.
Closed for refurbishment until late 2017.
Stations: Embankment. B.Cir.D. Waterloo. B.J.N.

■ **H.M.S. Belfast.** See "Belfast". ✪✪✪ ✪

■ **Horse Guards,** Whitehall. 4B 82 ✪✪✪ ✪
These barracks were rebuilt in 1753. Two mounted guardsmen are on sentry duty here, and the Changing of the Guard daily at 11 a.m., Sundays 10 a.m., is a picturesque sight. Trooping the Colour, a magnificent ceremony, takes place on the Queen's official birthday on the parade ground at the rear of the building.
Stations: Charing Cross. B.N. Westminster. Cir.D.J.

■ **Household Cavalry Museum,** Horse Guards. 4B 82
Illustrates over 300 years of the colourful history of the Sovereign's mounted bodyguard. Formed 1661 the Household Cavalry consists of the two most senior regiments of the British Army, The Life Guards and Royal Horse Guards (The Blues). *Admission Charge.*
Open: Daily 10 a.m. to 6 p.m. Winter 5 p.m. Closed Christmas and Good Friday. *Stations:* Charing Cross. B.N. Westminster. Cir.D.J.

■ **House of Illustration,** 2 Granary Square. 1B 62
Changing Exhibitions displaying all forms of the illustrators art, also talks, events and educational work.
Admission Charge. Open: 10 a.m. to 6 p.m. Tue. to Sun. Closed Monday and Christmas. *Station:* King's Cross St Pancras Cir.D.M.N.P.V.

■ **Houses of Parliament,** Parliament Square. 1C 94 ✪✪✪
Stand throughout the world as a symbol of democratic
government. Rebuilt in 1840 on the site of the Old Palace
of Westminster, which was destroyed by fire, this is the
largest building erected in England since the Reformation.
When Parliament sits, a flag flies from Victoria Tower by
day, and by night a light shines high in the famous 'Big
Ben' clock tower. To hear debates during Parliamentary
sittings, queue at the Cromwell Gardens visitor entrance;
UK residents may obtain advance tickets from their MP.
Guided tours every Saturday, and also most weekdays
during the Summer, Christmas and Easter recesses when
Parliament is not sitting. Tours are by timed ticket only from
ticket office, in advance by telephone 020 7219 4114, or
online. *Station:* Westminster. Cir.D.J.

■ **Huntarian Museum,** Royal College of Surgeons, 35-43
Lincoln's Inn Fields. 5E 71 Contains the oldest medical
collection in the world and aims to encourage exploration
of the scientific, cultural and historical importance of the
museum collections. Open: 10 a.m. to 5 p.m. Tues. to Sat.
Closed Sun. Mon. & Bank Holidays. *Station:* Holborn. C. P.

■ **Hyde Park.** 3B 78 ✪✪
This Royal Park covers 341 acres, and together with
Kensington Gardens forms an oasis of green tranquillity.
Features near Hyde Park Corner include The Holocaust
Memorial Garden and Rose Garden, near Marble Arch is
Speaker's Corner famous for its Sunday 'tub thumping'
public orators. The Serpentine lake has pleasure boats for
hire and the lido is open for swimming in Summer months.
The Diana, Princess of Wales Memorial Fountain is
located near the Serpentine Bridge. Horse riding takes
place on Rotten Row. *Stations:* Hyde Park Corner. P.
Knightsbridge. P. Lancaster Gate. Cen. Marble Arch. Cen.

■ **Imperial War Museum,** Lambeth Road. 3A 96 ✪✪✪ ✪
Records and illustrates all aspects of warfare, military and
civil, allied and enemy, in which Britain and the
Commonwealth have been involved since August 1914.
Besides the machinery of war there are photographic and
film records, printed materials, also dramatic recreations
including 'Trench Experience' and 'Blitz Experience' with
sounds, smells and special effects. The Holocaust
Exhibition uses historical artifacts and poignant displays to
explain the persecution of the Jews and other groups
before and during World War II.
Open: 10 a.m. to 6 p.m. daily. Closed 24,25,26 December.
Stations: Lambeth North. B. Elephant and Castle. B.N.

■ **Jack the Ripper Museum,** 12 Cable Street. 1F 87
An exhibition telling the history of East London in the

1880's with recreated rooms to display the gruesome story of the murder of the six women victims.
Admission Charge. Open: Daily 9.30 a.m. to 6.30 p.m.
Stations: Tower Hill Cir.D. Tower Gateway DLR.

■ ***Jewish Museum,** 129/131 Albert Street. off 1C 60
Illustrates British Jewish history, culture and faith; from silver, ivory, wood and textile antiquities to a complete recreation of an East End Jewish street.
Admission Charge.   Open: Daily 10 a.m. to 5 p.m. except 10 a.m to 2 p.m. Friday. Closed Dec. 25 and Jan. 1st. & Jewish Festivals. *Station:* Mornington Crescent. N.

■ **Kensington Gardens.** 3D 77 ✪✪
Formerly the grounds of Kensington Palace, now a woodland park where children gather at the Round Pond to sail their boats, visit the statue of Peter Pan and explore the Diana, Princess of Wales Memorial Playground – the 7 mile long memorial walkway passes nearby. The Long Water should be seen from the bridge that divides it from the Serpentine. The Serpentine Gallery has changing and challenging exhibitions of modern art. *Stations:* High Street Kensington. Cir.D. Lancaster Gate. Cen. Queensway. Cen.

■ **Kensington Palace,** Kensington Gardens. 4C 76 ✪✪
Designed by Wren for William III, Queen Victoria was born here and was the home of Diana, Princess of Wales. The Palace's State Apartments have been restored to reflect their former grandeur. Also themed exhibitions.
Admission Charge. Open: Daily 10 a.m. to 6 p.m. Summer. 10 a.m. to 5 p.m. Winter. Closed 24 - 26th December.
Stations: High Street Kensington. Cir.D. Queensway. Cen.

■ **Kew Gardens,** see Outer London. ✪✪

■ **Knightsbridge.** 1D 91 ✪
Famous area for high quality shopping, especially Harrods and Harvey Nichols.   *Station:* Knightsbridge. P.

■ **Lambeth Palace,** Lambeth Palace Road.
Has been for over 700 years the London residence of the Archbishop of Canterbury. Of particular interest is the historic public library founded in 1610 and freely open for research on application. Guided Tours available online.
Stations: Westminster Cir.D.J., Lambeth North. B.

■ **Lancaster House,** Stable Yard Road. 5D 81
This early Victorian mansion is known for the splendour of its State Apartments. Used for functions. *Stations:* Green Park. J.P.V., St. James's Park. Cir.D.

■ **Leadenhall Market,** Leadenhall Street. 5B 74
Victorian glass and Iron hall of 1881. Once specialised in poultry, now in quality delicatessen shops.
Station: Monument. Cir.D.

■ **Leicester Square.** 2A 82 ✪
Was laid out from 1635-70, and named after the Earl of Leicester, whose residence was on its north side. Hogarth and Joshua Reynolds also lived here.
Station: Leicester Square. N.P.

■ ***Leighton House Museum,** 12 Holland Park Road,
off 2A 88 Home and studio of the Victorian artist Frederic, Lord Leighton 1830-96, features include an amazing Arab Hall decorated with 13th-17th c. middle eastern tiles.
Admmission charge. Open daily 10 a.m. to 5.30 p.m. except closed Tuesdays. Closed Christmas Jan 1st.
Station: High Street Kensington Cir.D.

■ **Lincoln's Inn,** Chancery Lane. 4E 71 ✪
One of the four inns of Court which have the power of 'calling to the Bar'. The Law Library, built in 1845, is the finest in London and contains over 70,000 volumes and many fine MSS. Of particular interest are the early 16th century gateway to Chancery Lane and the Inigo Jones chapel consecrated in 1623.
Admission: To the Inn and Library on appointment. To the Chapel, free Sunday service 11.30 a.m., during sittings.
Stations: Chancery Lane. Cen. Holborn. Cen.P.

■ **Lloyd's,** Lime Street. 5B 74
This international insurance market and world centre of shipping intelligence is named after Edward Lloyd's coffee house, the 17th-century rendezvous of people interested in shipping. The exciting modern building has external observation lifts and service ducting in strong colours; the whole building being well and dramatically illuminated at night.
Stations: Aldgate. Cir.M. Bank. Cen.N. Monument. Cir.D

■ **Lombard Street.** 5A 74
Famous as the centre of banking, it owes its name to the Jewish Lombard goldsmiths and money-lenders who established themselves here after their expulsion in 1290.
Station: Bank. Cen.DLR.N.

■ **London Bridge.** 3A 86
There have been many bridges on this site, the first having been built by the Romans. The present bridge replaced the 1831 stone bridge, now in Lake Havasu City, Arizona U.S.A. *Stations:* London Bridge. J.N. Monument. Cir.D.

■ **London Bridge Experience,** Tooley Street. 3A 86 ✪ ✪
An exploration of the history of London Bridge from Roman and Medieval times together with London Tombs a horror make-believe experience.
Admission Charge. Open Mon. to Fri. 10 a.m. to 5 pm. Sat. & Sun. to 6 pm. *Station:* London Bridge. J.N.

■ **London Canal Museum,** New Wharf Road. IC 62
Tells the story of London's canals, including the role of
working horses; housed in what was an industrial ice
house built in the 1850's for Carlo Gatti the ice cream
manufacturer. *Admission Charge.*
Open: Tues. to Sun. and Bank Holiday Mondays 10 a.m. to
4.30 p.m. Closed on other Mondays and Christmas.
Station: King's Cross St. Pancras. Cir.D.P.N.V.M.H.

■ **London Dungeon,** Old County hall. 5D 83 ✪ ✪
An exhibition of gruesome and macabre events from the
Dark Ages until the end of the 17th century, not
recommended by the management to the nervous or
unaccompanied children. *Admission Charge.* Open: Daily.
Stations: Westminster. Cir.D.J. Waterloo. B.J.N.

■ **London Eye,** Old County Hall. 5D 83 ✪✪✪ ✪
The world's highest observation wheel provides
spectacular views over London from one of 32 enclosed
capsules. Gradual 30 minute ride reaches 450ft above the
River Thames. An iconic landmark and a symbol of
modern London. *Admission charge.* Open daily. Closed
Christmas Day and two weeks in January for maintainace.
Stations: Westminster. Cir.D.J. Waterloo. B.J.N.

■ **London Film Museum,** Wellington Street. 1C 82
Illustrating the history of movie making, interactive
displays, sets, costumes etc. Thematic special exhibitions.
Admission charge. Open daily. *Station:* Covent Garden. P.

■ **London Pavilion,** see Piccadilly Circus.

■ **London's Death Trap,** Old County Hall. 5D 83
Audio visual pseudo horror experience. *Admission charge,*
Open daily. *Stations:* Westminster. Cir.D.J. Waterloo. B.J.N

■ **London Sea Life Aquarium,** Old County Hall. 5D 83
✪✪ ✪ One of Europe's largest exhibits of fish and
marine life from around the world features huge Atlantic
and Pacific Ocean tanks. Also many other displays
including European and Exotic habitats, touch pools etc.
Admission Charge. Open Daily. Closed Christmas Day.
Station: Westminster. Cir.D.J.

■ **London Silver Vaults,** 53 Chancery Lane. 3F 71
Underground strongrooms built in the 1880s as a Safe
Depository. Now houses over 40 individual shops selling
all types of silverware from contemporary to antique and
Sheffield Plate. Open Monday to Friday and a.m. Saturday.
Station: Chancery Lane. Cen.

■ **London Transport Museum,** Covent Garden. 1C 82
✪✪ ✪ Historic vehicles and exhibits including early
steam and electric locomotives, horse-buses, motor buses
(including the famous 'B' type), tram cars, trolley buses,

posters, tickets, signs, etc. Sit in the driving seat of a London Bus or Underground Train; historical films show London as it was. Housed in a magnificent Victorian structure with cast iron arcades and glazed clerestories. *Admission Charge.* Open 10 a.m. to 6 p.m. Saturday to Thursday. 11 a.m to 6 p.m. Friday. Closed Christmas Day and Boxing Day *Station:* Covent Garden. P.

■ **London Zoo,** Regent's Park. 1F 59 ✪✪✪✪
The 'lure of the wild' in the heart of London; with over 750 species of animal this is a day out with a difference.
Special attractions include Land of the Lions new for 2016, Penguin Beach, Gorilla Kingdom, the walk through Tropical Jungle Bird Pavilion, Butterfly Paradise the Rainforest Lookout biome and Nightzone with its nocturnal animal displays. Animal Adventure, a childrens zoo experience allows children to immerse themselves in the sights, sounds and smells of life in the animal kingdom. Various animal encounters and animal feeding take place at certain times during the day.
Admission Charge. Open daily. Closes earlier in Winter months. Closed Christmas Day.
Stations: Camden Town. N. Regent's Park. B.

■ **Madame Tussaud's,** Marylebone Road. 1F 67 ✪✪✪✪
The world-famous waxwork exhibition and tourist attraction, where visitors wander among themed displays featuring life-like historical, showbiz and contemporary figures. *Admission charges vary.*
Open daily. Closed only on Christmas Day.
Station: Baker Street. B.Cir.J.M.H

■ **Mansion House.** 5F 73
Official home of the Lord Mayor of London, built in 1753 as one of London's grandest Georgian town palaces, the famous banquets given by the Lord Mayor take place in the Egyptian Hall. Tours of the magnificent interiors and historic treasures take place on Tuesdays 2 p.m. (closed August). *Admission charge. Station:* Bank. Cen. DLR.N.

■ **Marble Arch,** Oxford Street. 1E 79
Originally intended as an entrance to Buckingham Palace, this 'triumphal arch' was made too narrow for the State Coach and was utilised as a gate into Hyde Park. Later, the park boundary was moved back, leaving Marble Arch an entrance to nowhere. Nearby, where Edgware Road intersects Bayswater Road, stood Tyburn Gallows, where public executions took place until 1783.
Station: Marble Arch. Cen.

■ **Marlborough House,** Pall Mall. 4F 81
Built by Wren in 1709 for the Duke of Marlborough, it reverted to the Crown in 1817. Amongst its occupants

have been Edward VII when Prince of Wales, and George V until his accession. From 1911 until her death it was the residence of Queen Alexandra. Queen Mary lived here when in London. Now houses the Commonwealth Secretariat and hosts Commonwealth Conferences.

Adjoining the house is QUEEN'S CHAPEL 1627, designed by Inigo Jones. Services: Sun 8.30 and 11.15 a.m. Easter Day—end of July. *Station:* Green Park. J.P.V.

■ **MCC Cricket Tour & Museum,** Lord's Cricket Ground.
4A 58 Tours including entry to museum of cricket memorabilia and home of The Ashes. Regular tours daily, for advanced booking Tel 020 7616 8595. Restrictions apply on match days,
Admission Charge. *Station:* St. John's Wood. J.

■ **Monument, The.** 1A 86 ✪
A fluted Doric column erected by Sir Christopher Wren in the year 1677 to commemorate the Great Fire of London of 1666. Its height is 202 feet, which is the distance to the house in Pudding Lane where the fire broke out.
The magnificent view of the City from the top well repays the effort of ascending the 311 steps.
Admission Charge. Open daily 9.30 a.m. to 6 p.m; to 5.30 p.m. Winter months. *Station:* Monument. Cir.D.

■ ***Museum of Brands and Packaging,** 117 Lancaster Road, W11. History of consumer culture and shopping habits through printed material, packaging and advertising.
Admission charge. Open Tues. to Sat. 10 a.m to 6 p.m. Sundays 11 to 5 p.m. *Station:* Ladboke Grove. Cir.H.

■ **Museum of Childhood,** see Outer London.

■ **Museum of London,** London Wall. 3D 73 ✪ ✪
One of London's modern purpose-built museums: constructed as part of the Barbican. Imaginative displays include London before London; Roman London, Medieval London; Tudor & early Stuart London and Modern London, the story of London and its people from 1666 up to the present. See also Museum of London Docklands.
Open: Daily 10 a.m. to 6 p.m. Closed Christmas and Boxing Day. *Stations:* Barbican. Cir.M.H. St. Paul's. Cen

■ **Museum of Methodism,** see Wesley's House.

■ **Music Museum,** Royal Academy of Music, 1A 68
One of the finest collections of musical instruments maintained in playing condition, also archives, musical memorabilia and original manuscripts.
Open 11.30 a.m. to 5.30 p.m. Mon. to Fri. 12 noon to 4 p.m. Saturdays. Closed Sunday, Public Holidays and December. *Station:* Baker Street. B.Cir.J.M.H.

■ ***National Army Museum,** Royal Hospital Road, off Lower Sloane Street. SW3 5F 91. ✪ Museum of the British Army, and of the Indian Army to 1947 also colonial and auxiliary forces. Closed for refurbishment until late 2016. Open: 10 a.m. to 5.30 p.m. daily. Closed Good Friday, Christmas Eve and Day, Boxing Day and New Year's Day. *Station:* Sloane Square. Cir.D.

■ **National Gallery,** Trafalgar Square. 2A 82 ✪✪✪ The Gallery was opened in 1824 with the Angerstein Collection of 38 pictures, it has developed into one of the most important picture galleries in the world, containing a collection representative of every European school of painting and works by nearly all the Great Masters. In addition special exhibitions of great interest are mounted throughout the year. Open: 10 a.m. to 6 p.m. Friday to 9 p.m. Closed Christmas Eve and Day, Boxing Day and Good Friday. Free lectures on certain days. *Station:* Charing Cross. B.N.

■ **National Maritime Museum,** see Outer London. ✪✪✪✪

■ **National Portrait Gallery,** St. Martin's Place. 2A 82 ✪✪ National collection of painted and photographic portraits of famous British men and women dating mainly from the Tudor dynasty to the twentieth century. Special exhibitions throughout the year. Open: 10 a.m. to 6 p.m. daily. Thurs. and Fri. to 9pm. Closed 24, 25 and 26th December. *Stations:* Leicester Square. N.P. Charing Cross. B.N.

■ **National Theatre,** see South Bank Arts Centre

■ **Natural History Museum,** Cromwell Rd. 3F 89 ✪✪✪✪ One of the world's finest natural history collections; organised into *Blue and Green Zones*- dinosaurs, insects, ecology, human biology, mammals, sea life, origin of species etc and *Red Zones*- ancient and future earth, changing landcapes including an Earthquake Experience. *Orange Zone*- Darwin Centre enables visitors to see displays from the many millions of zoological specimens gathered by scientists for 400 years, talks and films in the Attenborough Studio. Activity sheets available for children. Open: 10 a.m. to 5.50 p.m. daily. Closed 24, 25, 26th December. *Station:* South Kensington. Cir.D.P.

■ **Newport Street Gallery,** Newport Street. 4E 95 Changing exhibitions of contemporary art. Open: 10 a.m. to 6 p.m. Closed Monday. *Stations:* Lambeth North. B. Vauxhall. V.

■ **Old Operating Theatre Museum,** 9a St. Thomas' St. 4F 85 An original Victorian operating theatre and Herb Garret, with instruments and apparatus illustrating medical history, and the history of St. Thomas's and Guy's Hospitals. *Admission Charge.* Open: 10.30 a.m. to 5 p.m. daily.

Station: London Bridge. J.N.

■ ***Olympia,** Hammersmith Road, W14.
It covers an area of 103/4 acres, and is one of the most famous showplaces and exhibition centres in the world.
Station: Kensington (Olympia). D. (Exhibitions only)

■ **Oxford Street.** 5B 68 ✪
One of Londons principal shopping streets, famous for its many department stores including Selfridges, John Lewis, Debenhams. Remarkably straight for London, it is on the site of the old Roman road leading west from the city.
Stations: Bond Street. Cen.J. Marble Arch. Cen. Oxford Circus. B.Cen.V. Tottenham Court Road. Cen.N.

■ **Oxo Tower Wharf,** South Bank 2A 84 ✪
A South Bank landmark, this imposing wharf is now a showpiece centre for artist designer-craftsmen; rooftop restaurant and 8th floor public viewing gallery.
See also Gabriel's Wharf nearby.
Stations: Waterloo. B.J.N. Blackfriars.Cir.D. Southwark. J.

■ **Petrie Museum,** University College. 1F 69
Egyptian and Sudanese archaeology illustrating life in the Nile Valley from prehistory through to the time of the pharaohs, the Ptolemaic, Roman Coptic and Islamic periods. Open: Tues to Sat. 1 to 5 p.m. Closed Christmas and Easter holidays. *Station:* Euston Square. Cir. M. H.

■ **'Petticoat Lane',** Middlesex Street. 3D 75 ✪
A street market for a numerous variety of goods where on Sunday mornings, bargain-hunters and passers-by are attracted to the stalls of persuasive salesmen.
Stations: Aldgate East. D.M., Liverpool Street. Cen.Cir.M.

■ **Photographers Gallery,** 16-18 Ramillies Street, 5D 69
Changing exhibitions by the latest emerging talent, historical archives and established artists. Talks, workshops and study room. Open: 10 a.m. to 6 p.m. Mon. to Sat. To 8 p.m. Thurs. during exhibitions. 11 a.m. to 6 p.m. Sun. *Station:* Oxford Circus. B. Cen. V.

■ **Piccadilly Circus.** 2F 81 ✪✪✪
A swirl of people, traffic and coloured lights; this is the traditional focal point of London. A pedestrian piazza links the famous Eros statue to the south side; both the Trocadero Centre and the London Pavilion provide traffic free environments of shopping and leisure facilities.
Station: Piccadilly Circus. B.P.

■ **Pollocks Toy Museum,** 1 Scala Street. 2E 69 ✪
Of particular interest to children of all ages. Toy theatres, games dolls, dolls' houses and toys, etc.
Admission Charge. Open: 10 a.m. to 5 p.m. Mon. to Sat. Closed Sun.and Bank Holidays. *Station:* Goodge Street. N.

■ ***Portobello Road Market,** Portobello Road, off Pembridge Road W11 2A 76. ✪
Famous for its Saturday market of antiques, Victoriana, pseudo-antiques, but the rest of the week Portobello and the surrounding streets are a lively mix of general market stalls, exotic food shops, fashion shops and restaurants.
Station: Ladbroke Grove. M. Westbourne Park. M.

■ **Postal Museum,** Phoenix Place. 5E 63
Opens late 2016 with interactive displays to show the development and importance of communications history, will feature rides on the underground Mail Rail railway.
Station: Chancery Lane. Cen.

■ **Queen's Gallery,** see Buckingham Palace. ✪

■ **Queen Victoria Memorial,** The Mall. 5D 81 ✪
Stands in front of Buckingham Palace. Of white marble the centre figure of the Queen is 13 ft high. Groups on the remaining sides represent Justice, Truth and Motherhood while the whole is surmounted by a winged Victory.
Stations: St. James's Park. Cir.D. Victoria. Cir.D.V. Green Park. J.P.V.

■ **Raven Row Gallery,** 56 Artillery Lane. 3D 75
Changing exhibitions of challenging contemporary art within an historic 18th c. Huguenot silk merchants shop.
Open: 11 a.m. to 6 pm. Wednesday to Sunday.
Station: Liverpool Street. Cen. Cir. M

■ **Regent's Park,** 2E 59 ✪✪
One of the largest London parks, this Royal Park covers an area of 472 acres and contains the Zoo and a large boating lake. Queen Mary's Gardens are famous for roses and the open-air theatre The formal Italianate Avenue Gardens contrast with the informal English Gardens.
Stations: Baker Street. B.Cir.J.M. Regent's Park. B.

■ **Regent Street.** 1D 81 ✪
This important shopping street was first designed by Nash in 1813 as a link between Carlton House and Regent's Park. It is now famous for its quality shops, fashion houses and department stores like Liberty and the toy emporium Hamleys.
Stations: Oxford Circus. B.Cen.V. Piccadilly Circus. B.P.

■ **Ripley's Believe It or Not!** London Pavilion. 2F 81
Collection of odd and bizarre objects from around the world. *Admission Charge.* Open: 10 a.m. to 12 a.m. daily.
Station: Piccadilly Circus. B.P

■ **Roman Amphitheatre,** see Guildhall

■ **Roosevelt Memorial,** Grosvenor Square. 1A 80
Britain's personal memorial to President Franklin D.

Roosevelt after the Second World War. 160,000 contributions of five shillings each closed the subscription list in less than 6 days. *Station:* Bond Street. Cen.J.

■ **Rose Playhouse,** 56 Park Street. 3E 85
Archaeological site of the first theatre on Bankside built 1587, and venue for Shakespeare plays before the opening of the nearby famous Globe Theatre. Programme of events. *Open 10 a.m. to 5 p.m. Saturday.*
Station: London Bridge. J.N

■ **Royal Academy of Arts,** Burlington House, Piccadilly.
2D 81 ✪✪✪ Founded by George III in 1768 with Sir Joshua Reynolds as its first President and located at Somerset House, the Academy moved here to the town house of the Earls of Burlington 1869. Many varied special exhibitions of great interest are held throughout the year, while the famous annual Summer Exhibition is of works for sale and by living artists and is open to all.
Admission Charge. Open: 10 a.m. to 6 p.m. daily, to 10.00 p.m. Friday. Closed Christmas.
Stations: Piccadilly Circus. B.P. Green Park. J.P.V.

■ **Royal Air Force Museum,** See Outer London. ✪✪ ✪

■ **Royal Albert Hall,** Kensington Gore. 1F 89 ✪
This largest Concert Hall in London, seating over 5,000 was completed in 1871. Home of the famous annual season of BBC Proms concerts.
Station: South Kensington. Cir. D.P.

■ **Royal College of Music Museum,** Prince Consort Road.
2F 89 The Royal College of Music museum of instruments contains an internationally renowned collection of over 800 instruments from c.1480 to present day. Open: Tues. to Fri. 11.30 a.m. to 4.30 p.m. *Station:* South Kensington. Cir.D.P.

■ **Royal College of Surgeons,** Lincoln's Inn Fields, 4E 71
Is the headquarters of surgery in England. Teaching, research and examinations are major functions of the College. For Huntarian Museum see above.
Station: Holborn. Cen.P.

■ **Royal Courts of Justice,** Strand, WC2. 5E 71
These buildings were opened in 1882, enlarged in 1911 and extended in 1968 and 1971. There are 50 Courts, and visitors are admitted to the public galleries. Courts generally sit in Term times: Weekdays, 10.30 a.m. to 4.30 p.m. Station: Temple. Cir.D.

■ **Royal Exchange,** Cornhill. 5A 74
Opened by Queen Victoria in 1844, the previous two buildings on this site burned down respectively in 1666 and 1838. Now a courtyard of shops and restaurants.
Station: Bank. Cen.DLR.N.

■ **Royal Festival Hall,** see South Banks Arts Centre.

■ **Royal Geographical Society,** Kensington Gore. 1F 89
Founded in 1830. Lowther Lodge was designed by
Norman Shaw 1874. Important cartographic library,
bibliographic archives and expedition relics.
*Changing exhibitions open 10 a.m. to 5 p.m. Mon. to Fri.
Closed Public Holidays and Christmas. Reading Room for
study and research, fees may apply.*
Station: Knightsbridge. P

■ ***Royal Hospital, Chelsea,** Royal Hospital Road, off Lower
Sloane Street, SW3. 5F 91* ✪
Was designed by Sir Christopher Wren and founded in
1682 by Charles II as a home for old soldiers. The 'Chelsea
Pensioner' is a well-known figure in his scarlet (Summer) or
dark blue (Winter) coat. The statue of Charles II in the
Figure Court is by Grinling Gibbons. In part of the spacious
gardens the Chelsea Flower Show is held annually by the
Royal Horticultural Society.
Open: **Museum** 10 a.m. to 4 p.m. Mon. to Fri. **Chapel** and
Great Hall 10 a.m. to 12 p.m. and 2 p.m. to 4 p.m. Mon. to
Sat. **The grounds** are open from 10 a.m. to dusk.
Station: Sloane Square. Cir.D.

■ **Royal Institution Faraday Museum,** Albermarle Street.
2D 81 The home of world changing science since 1799,
themed displays - experimentation, people and
communication include Faradays 1850's magnetic
laboratory and a current state-of-the-art nanotechnology
laboratory. Open Monday to Friday 9 a.m. to 6 p.m.
Stations: Green Park. J.P.V. Piccadilly Circus. B.P.

■ **Royal Mews,** see Buckingham Palace. ✪✪ ✪

■ **Royal Mint,** Tower Hill, 2E 87
It was here that our 'silver' and bronze coins were struck
between 1811 and 1970, work since transferred to
Llantrisant, South Wales. Prior to 1811 it was located in the
Tower of London. *Station:* Tower Hill. Cir.D.

■ **Royal Naval College,** see Outer London. ✪

■ **Royal National Theatre,** see National Theatre.

■ **Royal Opera House,** Bow Street, 5C 70
The home of the Royal Opera and Royal Ballet
companies, now fully modernised and restored with public
areas, exhibition spaces and restaurants.
Open Mon to Sat. *Station:* Covent Garden. P.

■ **Saatchi Gallery,** Duke of Yorks HQ, King's Road 5E 91
Besides changing exhibitions from the avant-garde
Saatchi Collection of modern art, the Gallery aims to
provide an innovative forum for contemporary art,
presenting work by largely unseen young artists or by

established international artists whose work has been rarely or never exhibited in the UK. Open daily 10 a.m. to 6 p.m. *Station:* Sloane Square. Cir. D.

■ **St. Bartholomew's Hospital and Museum,** Smithfield.
3C 72 Popularly known as 'Bart's', this is the oldest hospital in London, having been founded in 1123 by Rahere, together with an Augustine Priory, in the reign of Henry I. Its long history, artifacts and historic medical instruments are displayed in the Museum. Also in the hospital are portraits of famous physicians and surgeons by Reynolds, Lawrence, etc., and Hogarth's 'The Good Samaritan' and 'Pool of Bethesda'.
Admission charge: Open 10 a.m. to 4 p.m. Tues to Fri only. Closed Bank Hols. *Station:* St. Paul's. Cen.

■ **St. James's Palace.** 4E 81 ✪
Built in 1532 by Henry VIII on the site of a leper hospital, this Palace was from time to time used as a Royal Residence after the Palace of Whitehall had been burned down in 1698. Charles II, James II, Mary II and George IV were born here. It was from here that Charles I took leave of his children before walking across St. James's Park to his execution, outside the Banqueting House. The main gateway, the Tapestry and Armoury Rooms and the Chapel Royal are all that remain of the original building.
Admission: To the Chapel for the Sunday morning service at 8.30 a.m. and 11.15 a.m. October to Good Friday. See also Clarence House and Marlborough House.
Stations: Green Park. J.P.V., St. James's Park. Cir.D.

■ **St. James's Park.** 5F 81 ✪✪
These 93 acres were acquired by Henry VIII in 1531 to give him hunting near his Palace of Whitehall. It was under Charles II that the land was laid out into a formal garden by the French landscape gardener Le Notre. Redesigned by John Nash in the 1820's in the English landscape style into one of the most charming of London's Royal Parks. A variety of water birds inhabit the lake, and these may be identified by labelled reproductions.
Stations: St. James's Park. Cir.D., Charing Cross. B.N

■ **St. Katharine Docks,** St. Katharine-by-the-Tower. 2E 87
✪ Built 1827 to designs by Thomas Telford, these massive and secure warehouses were used to store valuable cargoes from all over the world. Historic structures have been restored and incorporated into a precinct of   shopping arcades, restaurants and cobbled walks around a 240 moorings Yacht Haven.
Station: Tower Hill. Cir.D. Tower Gateway. DLR.

■ **St. Martin-in-the-Fields,** St. Martin's Place 2B 82 ✪
This historic church rebuilt by James Gibbs 1721-61 is

famous as a landmark in Trafalgar Square, also for its work with the homeless and public concerts. Gift shop, Cafe in the Crypt and London Brass Rubbing Centre (see below) *Station:* Charing Cross. B.N.

■ **St. Paul's Cathedral,** St Paul's Churchyard. 5C 72 ✪✪✪
This is Sir Christopher Wren's masterpiece, built to replace the much larger Medieval Cathedral on the same site after its destruction in the Great Fire of 1666. The most prominent of London's buildings, this is an immense Renaissance structure, its exterior length being 515 ft, its width across transepts 250 ft., and the height from pavement to the top of the cross 365 ft. Together with many other chapels in St. Paul's there is the American Chapel, which was dedicated in the presence of Queen Elizabeth II and the then Vice-President Nixon of the United States. Among the many famous people buried here are Christopher Wren, Nelson, Wellington, Jellicoe, Reynolds and Turner. 627 steps lead to the Whispering Gallery, Stone Gallery and to the Great Ball.
Services held daily.
Open for visitors Mon. to Sat. 8.30 a.m. to 4 p.m. *Admission Charge for sightseers.* Visiting subject to restrictions during services and ceremonies. Open on Sundays for services only. *Station:* St. Paul's. Cen.

■ **Savoy Chapel,** Savoy Hill, Strand. 1D 83
The Queen's Chapel of the Savoy belongs to Her Majesty The Queen and is a private chapel of the Sovereign in her right as Duke of Lancaster. It does not fall within any bishop's jurisdiction, but remaining firmly within the Church of England; it is also the chapel of the Royal Victorian Order. The present Chapel was erected as part of a hospital founded under the will of Henry VII. It stands on the site of the old Palace of Savoy given to the Earl of Savoy by Henry III. Chaucer, it is believed, was married here during John of Gaunt's ownership. John of Gaunt had to flee, however when Wat Tyler's rebels destroyed the buildings in 1381. Open: Mon. to Thurs. 9 a.m. to 4 p.m. Sun. 9 a.m. to 1 p.m. Sun. service 11a.m. Closed August and September. *Station:* Embankment. B.Cir.D.N.

■ **Science Museum,** Exhibition Road. 3F 89 ✪✪✪ ✪
Renowned collection arranged in themed displays to illustrate the history of science and technology, development of engineering, transport and important industries. Among the great many iconic artifacts on display are the worlds first industrial steam engines, the locomotive 'Rocket', 'Penny-Farthing' cycle, Model T Ford motor car, the first trans-Atlantic aircraft, the experimental vertical take-off 'Flying Bedstead', Apollo 10 capsule. Other features include an IMAX cinema and many

interactive galleries for children like Launch Pad,
Open: daily 10 a.m. to 6 p.m. Closed 24, 25, 26
December. *Station:* South Kensington. Cir.D.P.

■ **Serpentine Gallery,** Kensington Gardens. 4A 78
■ **Serpentine Sackler Gallery,** Magazine building 3A 78.
Changing and challenging exhibitions of modern art.
Open daily 10 a.m. to 6 p.m. during exhibitions.
Stations: South Kensington. Cir.D.P. Lancaster Gate. Cen

■ **Shakespeare's Globe Theatre & Exhibition,** Bankside
3D 85 ✪✪ This reconstructed 1599 Globe Theatre, is
the first thatched building to be built in the centre of
London since the Great Fire 1666. Theatre Tour and
Exhibition devoted to Shakespeare and the London in
which he worked and lived is open throughout the year,
summer season of plays in the open air Globe Theatre.
Also here is the Sam Wanamaker Playhouse, a
reconstruction of an candle lit indoor Jacobean Theatre.
Globe Theatre tour & exhibition daily. Tours finish 12 noon
during the summer performance season. Closed 24 and
25th December. Tour and Exhibition Tel: 020 7902 1500.
Box Office 020 7401 9919. Enquiries 020 7902 1400.
Stations: London Bridge. J.N. Southwark. J.

■ **Shard, The,** St Thomas Street. 4A 86
At 1017ft Europe's tallest building wth offices, apartments,
hotel, restaurants and public viewing gallery.
Station: London Bridge. J.N.

■ **Sherlock Holmes Museum,** 221b Baker Street. 1E 67
Modelled on the life and times of Sherlock Holmes and Dr
Watson as portrayed by Sir Arthur Conan Doyle.
Admission Charge. Open 9.30 a.m. to 6 p.m. daily. Closed
25th Dec. *Station:* Baker Street. B.Cir.J.M.H.

■ **Shrek's Adventure,** Old County Hall. 5D 83
Family attraction and ride with Dreamworks animated
Shrek characters..
Admission Charge. Open daily. *Stations:* Westminster
Cir.D.J. Waterloo B.J.N.

■ **Sikorsky Museum,** 20 Princes Gate. 1A 90. Collection of
Polish Institute and Sikosky memorabilia. Open Tues. to
Fri, 2 p.m. to 4 p.m. *Station:* South Kensington. Cir.D.P.

■ **Sir John Soane's Museum,** Lincoln's Inn Fields. 3E 71 ✪
This house was designed and built in 1812 by Sir John
Soane, architect to the Bank of England, to contain his own
museum, furniture, and library. Among the many unique
exhibits are Egyptian, Greek and Roman antiquities,
including the Sarcophagus of Seti 1; paintings by
Canaletto, Watteau and Reynolds; and the finest collection
of Hogarth's work, comprising the eight scenes of 'The

Rake's Progress' and four of 'The Election'.
Open: Tuesday to Saturday, 10 a.m. to 5 p.m. Closed Sun.
Mon. and Bank Holidays. *Station:* Holborn. Cen.P.

■ **Smithfield.** 3C 72
Now chiefly known for its Meat Market. In the past, the
'smooth field' lying outside the city wall was variously used
for jousting, for St. Bartholomew's Fair (held annually for
centuries), and for many executions. Among those
executed here were: William Wallace, beheaded in 1305
for supporting Robert Bruce's claim to the Scottish throne.
Roman Catholic and Protestant Martyrs burnt at the
stake—during the 16th and early 17th centuries—for their
beliefs. Wat Tyler was struck dead in 1381 by the Lord
Mayor, helping to bring the Peasants Revolt to an end.
Stations: Barbican. Cir.M. Farringdon. Cir.M.

■ **Somerset House,** Strand and Victoria Embankment 1D 83
✪✪ Like a huge palace around a central square,
Somerset House was built 1776-86 in grand neo classical
style by Sir William Chambers on the site of the 16th c.
palace of the Duke of Somerset.
The building once housed the Navy Board, the Royal
Academy and Royal Society, more recently the Inland
Revenue and General Register Office.
The Courtyard with its fountain display, is now a public
open space and events venue. The **Courtauld Gallery**
occupies the Strand side. The Visitor Centre, Embankment
Galleries, restaurants and 800ft. river front terrace make up
the south side, a Navy Commissioners Barge is displayed
in the original Water Gate entrance. *Admission charges,*
Visitor Centre free. Open: 10 am to 6 pm. extended
evenings for courtyard, river front terrace and restaurants.
Stations: Temple. Cir.D. Charing Cross. B.N.

■ **Sotheby's,** 34/5 New Bond Street. 1C 80
Founded in 1744 it is one of the oldest and largest firms of
fine art auctioneers. Sales of furniture, jewellery, silver,
porcelain, pictures, books etc., held regularly except in
August. Telephone 020 7293 5000 for details.
Station: Bond Street. Cen. J.

■ **South Bank Arts Centre.** 3E 83 ✪✪
One of Londons premier centres of cultural excellence on
the site of the 1951 Festival of Britain. Visit the Royal
Festival Hall, the National Theatre and BFI Southbank,
each has a foyer open daily with cafes, bookshops and
exhibitions; also here are the Hayward Gallery (closed until
2017) and BFI IMAX cinema. Spacious riverside terraces
offer an extensive choice of restaurants and the South
Bank Book Market.
Stations: Embankment. B.Cir.D.N. Waterloo. B.J.N.

■ **Southwark Cathedral,** London Bridge. 3F 85 ⭐⭐
This fine Gothic edifice built upon a nunnery, was originally the church of an Augustinian Priory, founded under Henry I. John Harvard, founder of Harvard University, U.S.A., was baptised here in 1607. Exactly 300 years later a chapel and window were erected in his memory by Harvard students. Fletcher, Massinger and Edmund Shakespeare—brother of William—are buried here.
Open daily. *Station:* London Bridge. J.N.

■ **Spencer House,** 27 St. James's Place. 4D 81 ⭐
London's finest surviving 18th century Town House, built 1756-66 for the first Earl Spencer, an ancestor of the late Diana, Princess of Wales. *Admission Charge.* Open: Sundays only 10.30 a.m. to 4.45 p.m. closed Aug. and Jan. Access by guided tour only. *Station:* Green Park. P.V

■ **Spitalfields Market,** Commercial Street. 2D 75
This historic fruit and vegetable market is now the centre of a renewed Spitalfields area with its restaurants, shops and popular Sunday market.
Station: Liverpool Street. Cen.Cir.H.M

■ **18 Stafford Terrace.** 2A 88
Victorian interiors as created for the 'Punch'. cartoonist Linley Sambourne. *Admission Charge.* Open: Wed. Sat. and Sun p.m. also via bookable guided tours Tel: 020 7602 3316 Mon. to Fri. *Station:* High Street Kensington. Cir.D.

■ **Staple Inn,** Holborn. 3F 71
Staple Inn was formerly one of the lesser Inns of Court and described by Charles Dickens in his novel 'Edwin Drood'. His Mr. Grewgious lived here, and so in real life did Dr. Johnson. *Station:* Chancery Lane. Cen.

■ **Tate Britain,** Millbank. 5B 94 ⭐⭐⭐
The national gallery of British art from 1500 to the present, from the Tudors to the Turner prize. This most comprehesive collection of British art in the world includes works by Blake, Constable, Epstein, Gainsborough, Hogarth, Lely, Kneller, Stubbs, the Pre Raphaelites, Spencer, Moore, Hockney and most notably the Turner bequest in its own wing, the Clore Gallery.
Also special exhibitions and retrospectives.
Open: 10 am to 6 pm daily. Closed 24th -26th December.
Station: Pimlico. V.

■ **Tate Modern,** Bankside. 3C 84 ⭐⭐⭐
Housed in the transformed former Bankside Power Station is the Tate's collection of international modern art from 1900 to the present. It includes works by over 200 artists including Auerbach, Bacon, Braque, Cragg, Duchamp, Giacometti, Matisse, Picasso, Riley, Rothko, Warhol and many contemporary and controversial artists. Also special

exhibitions and retrospectives.   Roof top restaurant with panoramic views over the City of London.
Open: 10 a.m. to 6 p.m. daily, 10 a.m. to 10 p.m. Friday and Saturday. Closed 24th - 26th December.
Stations: Southwark. J. Blackfriars. Cir.D.

■ **Temple,** Fleet Street. 1F 83 **✪✪**
A complex of quiet squares and courts, of quaint corners, these precincts preserve a remarkable feel of 'old London'. Formerly the property of the Knights Templars—from 1184 to 1313—and then of the Knights of St. John of Jerusalem; it finally came into the possession of two Inns of Court—Inner Temple and Middle Temple. Open: Middle Temple Hall 10 a.m. to 12 p.m. and 3 to 4 p.m. Mon. to Fri. only. Temple Church generally open daily.   All closed for public holidays. *Station:* Temple. Cir.D.

■ **Temple Bar,** Strand. 5F 71
Historically the western entrance to the City of London; when the Sovereign visits the City she is met here by the Lord Mayor of London, a Griffin Monument marks the site.
Station: Temple Cir.D.
The imposing **Temple Bar Gate** designed by Wren in 1672 and removed in 1878, is now sited between St Paul's Cathedral and Paternoster Square. 5C 72
Station: St Paul's. C.

■ **Tower Bridge Exhibition.** Tower Bridge. 3D 87
✪✪✪ ✪   Discover the history of Tower Bridge, how it works, London in the 1890's, and enjoy the spectacular views from the 142 ft high walkways. Tower Bridge, one of the sights of London, was designed by Barry and Jones and completed in 1894, the two draw-bridges open to allow the passage of large ships, a bell rings before the bridge opens, halting all traffic.
Admission Charge. Open 10 a.m. to 5.30 p.m. Summer months. 9.30 a.m. to 5 p.m. Winter months. Closed 24-26 December. *Stations:* Tower Hill. Cir.D. Tower Gateway. DLR.

■ **Tower of London.** 2D 87 **✪✪✪ ✪**
Built in part by William the Conqueror in 1078 as a fortress to guard the river approach to London, this is the most perfect example of a medieval castle in England, the outer walls being added later.
  The White Tower contains, besides its collection of firearms and execution relics, the finest early-Norman chapel in this country. The famous Crown Jewels are housed in Waterloo Block. Elsewhere is the Royal Fusiliers Museum. Wall Walk gives good views over the Tower and River.
Anne Boleyn, Katherine Howard, Lady Jane Grey, Margaret Countess of Salisbury, Jane Viscountess

Rochford, Robert Devereux Earl of Essex, were executed on Tower Green.
Admission Charge. Open *Summer:* 9 a.m. to 5.30 p.m. Tues. to Sat. 10 a.m. to 5.30 pm. Sun. and Mon. *Winter:* 9 am to 4.30 pm. Tues to Sat. 10 am. to 4.30 pm. Sun. and Mon. Closed 24-25th December, New Year's Day.
To book tickets advance Tel. 0844 482 7799.
Stations: Tower Hill. Cir.D. Tower Gateway. DLR.

■ **Trafalgar Square. 3A 82 ✪✪✪**
Laid out as a war memorial and named after the victory of Trafalgar, the Square was completed in 1841. Nelson's Column, 170 ft. high overall, traditionally allowing Nelson a view of the sea. The lions at the base are by Landseer, facing Whitehall is a 17th-century equestrian statue of Charles I, the Martyr King. *Station:* Charing Cross. B.N.

■ **Two Temple Place,** 2 Temple Place. 1F 83
Extravagant neo-Gothic mansion built for William Waldorf Astor. Displays periodic loan exhibitions. Open: (execept during changes of exhibition) daily- but closed Tuesday. *Station:* Temple. C.D

■ **UCL Art Museum,** South Cloisters, University College London. 5F 61 Periodic exhibitions from the rich collection associated with the Slade School of Fine Art..
Open: (except between changes of exhibition). 1pm and 5pm from Mon. to Fri. *Station:* Euston Square Cir.M.H

■ **University of London,** Russell Square. 2A 70
This Senate House, completed just before the Second World War, contains the University Library and central administration. Many of the Schools and Institutes constituting the University, like University College, are located nearby; with others throughout the London area, and some beyond. *Station:* Russell Square. P.

■ **Victoria and Albert Museum,** Cromwell Road. 3A 90 ✪✪✪ One of the worlds great museums of fine and applied art. It illustrates artistic achievement and craftsmanship throughout the centuries and is arranged into two groups (a) Primary Collections—of style, period or nationality. (b) Departmental Collections— sculpture, textiles, woodwork, etc.
Many galleries now benefit from world class modern presentation including the British Galleries, Medieval and Renaissance Galleries, Ceramics, Furniture, Jewellery, Sculpture and Theatre Galleries. Special exhibitions occur throughout the year. The museum incorporates the National Art Library.
Open 10 a.m. to 5.45 p.m. daily. To 10 pm Fridays (note: selected galleries after 6pm). Closed 24-26 December.
Station: South Kensington. Cir.D.P.

■ **Vinopolis,** Bankside. 3E 85
Exhibition and multi-media tour of the worlds wines, wine tastings, shops, restaurants. Admission charge. Open Wed. to Sun. p.m. only . *Station:* London Bridge. J.N.

■ **Wallace Collection,** Hertford House, Manchester Square. 4F 67 ✪ The most representative collection in England of French 18th-century painting, sculpture, furniture and Sevres porcelain. It includes masterpieces by Rembrandt, Hals, Rubens, Reynolds, Gainsborough, Van Dyck, Velasquez and Titian; important collections of ceramics, goldsmiths' work, and European and Oriental arms and armour. Formed in the main by the third and fourth Marquesses of Hertford and the latter's son, Sir Richard Wallace. Open: Daily 10 a.m. to 5 p.m. Closed 24 -26 December.
Stations: Bond Street. Cen.J., Baker Street. B.Cir.J.M.

■ **Wellcome Collection,** 183 Euston Road. 5F 61
Explores the culture of medicine through the arts, sciences and history through both permanent and temporary exhibitions. The Welcome Library is one of the world's greatest collections for the study of the history and progress of medicine. Open: Tues. to Sat. 10 a.m. to 6 p.m. Thurs. to 10 p.m. Sun. 11 to 6. Library closed Sunday.
Station: Euston Square Cir.M.H

■ **Wellington Arch,** Hyde Park Corner. 5A 80
Designed by Decimus Burton in 1828. Originally a statue of Wellington stood on top, this was replaced by the present group when the Arch was moved from the entrance to Hyde Park. The frieze is based on the Elgin Marbles to be seen in the British Museum.
Admission Charge. Open: Visitor Centre Exhibition and Viewing Platform 10 a.m. to 5 p.m. (4 p.m. winter months). Closed Christmas and New Year.
Station: Hyde Park Corner. P.

■ **Wellington Museum,** see Apsley House.

■ **Wesley's House, Chapel and Museum of Methodism**
City Road. 1A 74   John Wesley lived here for 12 years and died in this house in 1791. His own rooms and furniture are preserved, and the Museum contains a unique collection of his possessions. Wesley is buried in the graveyard behind the Chapel.
Admission Charge. Open 10 a.m. to 4 p.m. Mon. to Sat. Closed Bank Hols. Chapel is also open for Sunday services. *Stations:* Old Street. N. Moorgate. Cir.M.N

■ **Westminster Abbey,** Parliament Square. 2B 94 ✪✪✪
One of the most interesting and historic religious buildings in England, its origins go back to the founding of an Augustinian monastery by St Dunstan c. AD 960, Edward

the Confessor added a new Abbey church consecrated 1065. Rebuilding in the Gothic style began under Henry III in 1245, the Choir and east end being rededicated 1269. The nave (at 102ft England's highest Gothic vault) dates from the late 13th and early 14th centuries. Major additions to the medieval work are the Henry VII Chapel 1503-19 with its awe inspiring fan vault roof and the twin West Towers - 18th century additions by Nicholas Hawksmoor, a pupil of Wren.

Until George III most of the Kings of England were buried within its precincts. Almost all have been crowned here; the only two exceptions being Edward V, who was murdered before he could be crowned, and the Duke of Windsor, Edward VI who abdicated in 1936.

Many famous men are buried in the Abbey, there is the well known Poets Corner, and the grave of the Unknown Warrior. The Abbey Museum in the outstanding Norman Undercroft shows the history and a remarkable collection of Royal and Noble effigies and death masks.

Open: Nave, Royal Chapels, Poets' Corner, Choir, and Statesmens' Aisle, Chapter House and Museum open Monday to Saturday. Cloisters open daily.
Admission Charge for sightseers.
Visiting subject to restrictions during special services and ceremonies. Open on Sundays for services only.
Stations: Westminster. Cir.D.J. St. James's Park. Cir.D.

■ **Westminster R.C. Cathedral,** Ashley Place. 3E 93 ✪✪
Opened in 1903, this is the foremost Roman Catholic Church in England. The architect, John Francis Bentley, who was influenced by the Christian Byzantine style of St Sophia at Constantinople, died a year before the building was completed. A lift serves the Campanile, which is 284 ft. high. In May 1982 Pope John Paul II celebrated the first mass ever by a Pope on English soil.
Open 7 a.m. to 7 p.m. daily. Admission Charge for lift to viewing gallery, open 9.30 a.m to 5 p.m. Monday to Friday. 9.30 a.m. to 6 p.m. weekends. *Station:* Victoria. Cir.D.V.

■ **Westminster Hall,** Parliament Square. 1B 94 ✪
The main surviving fragment of the old Palace of Westminster destroyed by fire in 1834. Erected in 1097 by William Rufus, it was rebuilt 1394-99 by Richard II who was responsible for the magnificent oak roof spanning the width of the Hall. Many famous State trials have taken place here; among them those of Charles I, Sir Thomas More, Guy Fawkes and Warren Hastings. Now used for great functions and for 'Lying in State'.
Normally accessible via tours of the Houses of Parliament, see above for details.
Station: Westminster. Cir.D.J.

■ **Whitechapel Art Gallery,** Whitechapel High Street, 4E 75
Exhibitions of modern and contemporary art, and
showcase for new artists. Established in 1901 to bring art
to the then culturally deprived 'East End', The gallery is an
important Arts and Crafts building.
Admission Charge. Open Tues. to Sun 11 a.m. to 6 p.m.
Thus. to 9 p.m. *Station:* Aldgate East. D.M.H.

■ **Whitehall.** 4B 82 ✪✪✪
Part of the original palace of Whitehall, this famous
thoroughfare extends from Trafalgar Square southwards to
Parliament Square. At the entrance to the Horse Guards
Parade, mounted guards are on sentry duty.
Downing Street, home of the Prime Minister, is a turning off
Whitehall near the Cenotaph, the principal monument in
the centre of the road. Many Government Departments are
housed here.
Stations: Charing Cross. B.N. Westminster. Cir.D.J.

PLACES OF INTEREST, MUSEUMS and ART GALLERIES in OUTER LONDON

■ *NOTE: These items are all outside the central area map.*
Many can be most easily visited by taking an appropriate
coach tour, see Conducted Coach Tours.

■ **Brunel Museum,** Railway Avenue, Rotherhithe SE16.
The history of the worlds first under river tunnel, also the
lives of the Brunel's, father and son. *Admission Charge.*
Open: daily 10 a.m. to 5 p.m. *Station:* Rotherhithe. O.

■ **Chartwell,** near Westerham, Kent ✪
For many years the country home of Sir Winston Churchill;
the house is maintained as he left it, as is the studio where
many of his paintings were executed. There are extensive
gardens.   Now a National Trust Property.
Admission Charge. Open: House, March to end October
11 a.m. to 5 p.m. Garden, daily 10 a.m. to 5 p.m. closed
24th and 25th December.

■ **Chessington World of Adventures,** Leatherhead Road,
Chessington, Surrey. ✪ ✪   Theme Park and Fun Fair
with over 100 attractions and rides; also zoo and skyway
monorail.   *Admission Charge:* Fully open at peak times
and on Zoo Days. Check for opening times online or
Telephone 0871 663 4477. *Station:* Chessington South by
train from Waterloo.

■ **Chiswick House,** Burlington Lane W4 ✪
A fine example of Palladian architecture built by the Third
Earl of Burlington in the late 1720's, its frontage composed
of two double approach stairways flanking a classical
portico at first floor level. The interior with its series of

34

connected rooms designed by William Kent has fine paintings, sculpture and furniture. The garden laid out by Kent was a forerunner to the English Landscape Park. *Admission Charge.* Open: House, March to October 10 a.m. to 6 p.m. Sunday to Wednesday & Bank Holidays. Garden, open daily.
Station: Chiswick by train from Waterloo.

■ **Cutty Sark,** Greenwich, SE10 ✪✪✪ ✪
Built in 1869, this was the fastest and most famous of the clipper sailing ships that raced to bring their tea cargoes to British ports. After complete restoration, the ships raised position enables visitors to walk underneath and examine the shape of the hull. Interpretive exhibitions explore the history of the ship and the tea trade, and includes the world's largest collection of Merchant Navy figureheads. Part of the National Maritime Museum.
Admission Charge. Open: 10 a.m. to 5 p.m. daily.
Station: See the National Maritime Museum.

■ **Docklands**
The Port of London was once one of the worlds largest ports occupying the banks of the River Thames from the Tower of London to Woolwich; during the 1960's and 70's industrial strife and new technologies bought about their decline and replacement by modern facilities at Tilbury.
    Since then some eight and a half square miles of derelict or underused land and water has undergone a remarkable transformation.
    Among the areas of interest are St. Katharine Docks, Canary Wharf Financial Centre, New Billingsgate Fish Market, London City Airport, The Thames Barrier and the dockside ExCeL state-of-the-art international event venue and The O2 arena. **See also Museum of London Docklands.**

■ **Dulwich Picture Gallery,** College Road, SE21 ✪
An outstanding collection of Flemish, Italian and Dutch Art. Paintings by Ruisdael, Van de Velde, Cuyp, Van Dyck, Rembrandt, Rubens, Claude, Raphael, Veronese, Murillo and Poussin, it also contains British 17th and 18th century portraiture, including Gainsborough and Reynolds. Special exhibitions of great interest throughout the year.
Admission Charge. Open: Tues. to Sun. 10 a.m. to 5 p.m. Closed Mon. except Bank Holiday Mondays. Closed Christmas and New Year. *Stations:* North Dulwich by train from London Bridge or West Dulwich from Victoria.

■ **Eltham Palace,** Court Yard, Etham. ✪✪✪
A unique and spectacular Art Deco house, built for the Courtaulds in 1936, linked to the Great Hall with its massive hammerbeam roof built in the 1470's and other remains of the Medieval Palace; set in beautiful gardens.

Admission Charge. Open Sun. to Thus. 10 a.m. to 6 p.m. summer months. 10am to 4pm winter months on restricted days. Closed Christmas and all January.
Station: Eltham or Mottingham from Victoria +15 min walk.

■ **Emirates Air Line Cable Car**
A Cable car ride across the river Thames linking stations at Greenwich Peninsula and The Royal Victoria Docks for pedestrians and cyclists.
Stations: North Greenwich J. Royal Victoria DLR

■ **Epping Forest,** Between Chingford and Epping
A relic of the ancient Royal hunting forest of Waltham. Now extending about 11 miles north/south, by 2-3 miles across, and managed by the City of London Corporation providing free public access at all times. Epping Forest Museum is in Queen Elizabeth's Hunting Lodge, Rangers Road, E14.
Station: Chingford by train from Liverpool Street.

■ **Estorick Collection of Modern Art,** 39a Canonbury Square, N1 A museum of modern Italian Art including the finest collection of Futurist Paintings outside Italy. *Admission Charge.* Open Wed to Sat. 11a.m. to 6 p.m. Sun.12 to 5 p.m. Closed Mon. & Tues.
Station: Highbury & Islington. V.

■ **Fan Museum,** 12 Crooms Hill, Greenwich SE10
Is the world's first and only museum of fans; elegant displays in a fine early Georgian house with Orangery and landscape garden. *Admission Charge.* Open: 11 a.m. to 5 p.m. Tues. to Sat. From 12 p.m. Sundays. Closed Mon.
Station: See the National Maritime Museum.

■ **Firepower, Museum of the Royal Artillery.** Royal Arsenal, Woolwich SE18 The story of Artillery and the history of the Royal Arsenal. *Admission Charge.* Open 10 a.m. to 5 p.m. Tues. to Sat. Closed Sun. and Mon. *Station: Woolwich Arsenal from Charing Cross.*

■ **Freud Museum,** 20 Maresfield Gardens, Hampstead NW3
The study of the founder of psychoanalysis is kept exactly as it was in his lifetime, including his library, antiquities and the famous couch. *Admission Charge.* Open: 12 am. to 5 p.m. Wed. to Sun. *Station:* Swiss Cottage. J.

■ **Fulham Palace Museum,** Bishops Avenue, SW6
Illustrates the history of the Palace. The site, first acquired by Bishop Waldhere in 704, was the residence of the Bishops of London until 1973. Open: Summer: Sun. to Thurs. 12.30 to 4.30 p.m. Winter: 12.30 to 3.30 p.m.
Station: Putney Bridge. D.

■ **Greenwich,**
For **Discover Greenwich Visitor Centre** see Royal Naval College. See also Cutty Sark, National Maritime Museum,

Queen's House and Royal Observatory.

■ **Hampton Court Palace,** Hampton, Middlesex ✪✪✪
Built by Cardinal Wolsey in 1515, and at that time the largest and most magnificent palace in England, it aroused Henry VIII's envy and concern. Ten years later it was presented to him by the Cardinal, and from then until George II, remained a favourite Royal residence.
Set around the three principal courtyards, visitors can explore The Wolsey Rooms, Henry VIII's State Appartments and Chapel, the extensive Tudor Kitchens, William III's State and private apartments etc. The Renaissance Picture Gallery displays important works from the Royal Art Collection. There are over 60 acres of grounds and gardens, which include the Privy Garden, the Orangery by Wren and the famous Maze.
Admission Charge. Open: daily 10 a.m. to 6 p.m. Summer months.10am to 4.30 p.m. winter months. Closed 24-26 Dec. *Station:* Hampton Court by train from Waterloo Station. Or in summer, by riverboat from Westminster Pier.

■ **Hampstead Heath,** Hampstead, NW3
A great tract of undulating, informal parkland, among its many delights are Parliament Hill, with its kite flyers and superb views over London. See also Kenwood.
Open daily. Station: Hampstead. N.

■ **Hogarth's House,** Hogarth Lane, W14.
The Queen Anne style country home of the artist Hogarth, now a museum of his drawings and engravings.
Open: Tues. to Sun. 12 noon to 5 p.m. Closed Mon. Christmas and Easter. *Station:* Turnham Green. D. P.

■ **Horniman Museum,** 100 London Road, SE23. ✪ ✪
Home to the most comprehensive musical instrument collection in Britain, the museum has an internationally renowned anthropological collection and a popular Natural History Gallery featuring rare fossils and natural specimens. The gardens with their stunning views over London are an award winning mix of garden types.
Open: 10.30 a.m. to 5.30 p.m. daily. Closed 24-26 Dec. *Station:* Forest Hill by train from Charing Cross or London Bridge.

■ **Keats House,** Wentworth Place, Keats Grove, NW3.
Keats Regency home between 1818-20. Now a museum of personal relics. Open: Summer 1 to 5 p.m. Tues. to Sun. Winter reduced opening hours. *Station:* Hampstead. N.

■ **Kenwood,** Hampstead, NW3 ✪✪
A classical style mansion set in 24 acres of parkland once owned by the first Earl of Mansfield. Designed by Robert Adam 1767-9 with additions by Saunders in 1795. Bequeathed to the Nation by the late Lord Iveagh in 1927,

complete with his fine collection of paintings and furniture.
Lakeside open air concerts held in the summer.
Open: Daily 10 a.m. to 5 p.m. Closed 24-26 Dec. 1st Jan.
Park open 8 a.m. to dusk. *Station:* Archway N. then Bus.

■ **Kew Gardens,** Royal Botanic Gardens, Kew, Surrey.
✪✪✪ Beautifully situated by the Thames; contain over
25,000 different species and varieties of trees shrubs and
plants from all over the world in 300 acres of landscape.
The great many special features include two museums, an
art gallery dedicated to botanical art, a magnificent Palm
House, Lily House, Rhododendron Walk, Kew Palace and
Princess of Wales Conservatory. *Admission Charge.*
Open: Daily from 10 a.m. Closed 24 and 25th December.
Stations: Kew Gardens. D. or Kew Bridge by train from
Waterloo. In summer, by riverboat from Westminster Pier.

■ **Legoland,** Windsor Park, Windsor , Berkshire. ✪
Theme park for children, built from and around the lego
building block theme; rides, set display pieces and
attractions in 150 acres of parkland.
Admission Charge. Open: hours very during the season.
Closed Winter months. Check online or Tel: 0871 222
2001. *Stations:* Windsor and Eton Central from Paddington,
via Slough; or Windsor and Eton Riverside from Waterloo;
then Legoland shuttle bus.

■ **London Museum of Water and Steam,** Green Dragon
Lane, Brentford. ✪ Worlds largest collection of steam
pumping engines together with related exhibitions and
events. *Admission Charge.* Open: 11 a.m. to 4 p.m. 'In
Steam' weekends and Bank Holidays.
Station: Kew Bridge by train from Waterloo.

■ **Museum of Childhood,** Cambridge Heath Road, Bethnal
Green E2. ✪ ✪ This branch of the Victoria and Albert
Museum has outstanding collections of toys, games, dolls
and dolls' houses; also children's costume; many activities
for children. Open: 10 a.m. to 5.45 p.m. daily. Closed 25-
26 Dec. 1st Jan. *Station:* Bethnal Green. Cen.

■ **Museum of London Docklands,** West India Quay,
Hertmere Road E14 Tells the story of London's river and
the importance of its trading port from Roman times
onwards; 2000 years of history explored in interactive
displays and historic artifacts.
Admission charge. Open 10 a.m. to 6 p.m., daily. Closed
24-26 Dec. *Station:* West India Quay. DLR.

■ **Museum of Richmond,** Old Town Hall, Whittaker Avenue,
Richmond. Illustrates the long history of Richmond.
Open: 11 a.m. to 5 p.m. Tues. to Fri. to 4 p.m. Sat. Closed
Public Holidays. *Station:* Richmond. D. or by train from
Waterloo.

■ **National Achives,** Ruskin Avenue, Kew, Richmond, Surrey TW9 4DU. Houses the National Archives accumulated since the Norman Conquest, including records created and acquired by the government. The Keeper's Gallery mounts changing exhibitions featuring the nation's most famous documents and unique items of historical interest.
Open: Keeper's Gallery 9 a.m. to 5 p.m. Tuesday. to Saturday. Reading rooms are open to the public Wednesday, Friday and Saturday 9 am. to 5 pm. (last call for documents 4.15 pm.); Tuesday and Thursday 9 am. to 7 pm. (last call 5 pm.). Closed Sunday and Monday, Bank Holidays and also Saturdays on Bank Holiday weekends. For information on viewing documents Tel: 020 8876 3444 or online.
Stations: Kew Gardens. D. or Kew Bridge by train from Waterloo Main Line Station.

■ **National Maritime Museum,** Greenwich, SE10 ✪✪✪✪
The National Museum of our maritime history dealing with every aspect of ships and seafaring both in peace and war, from prehistory to today. Exhibitions tell the story of historical events and important people, exploration and the world's oceans.
Besides the collections of ships models and works of art there are 'hands-on' interactive galleries for children. See also Cutty Sark, Queen's House and Royal Observatory.
Open: 10 am. to 5 pm. daily. *Station:* Greenwich by train from Cannon Street or (London Bridge, except between Aug. 2016 - Jan. 2018). Or Docklands Light Railway to Cutty Sark Station. Or by riverboat from Westminster or Tower Pier.

■ **Osterley Park House,** off Jersey Road, Isleworth.
A National Trust property. The house was begun in the 1560's as an Elizabethan Mansion for Sir Thomas Gresham, founder of the Royal Exchange. Later remodelled by both William Chambers and Robert Adam. Besides adding the portico, Adam designed the magnificent interiors and matching furniture. Outside are stables, parkland and the elevated M4 motorway !
Admission Charge. Open: Wednesday to Sunday. 11 a.m. to 5 p.m. March. to October. Park daily.
Station: Osterley. P.

■ **Queen's House,** National Maritime Museum, Greenwich, SE10. ✪ Commissioned by James 1st, this Palace is a design by Inigo Jones, which, with his Banqueting House, Whitehall, marks the introduction of the classical ideals of Palladian architecture into England.
Notable for its Great Hall, a huge 40ft cube with a fine black-and-white marble floor and the elegant Tulip Stairs,

the first geometric self-supporting spiral stair in Britain.
Displays the museums maritime fine art collection.
Open and Station: as the National Maritime Museum.

■ **Ragged School Museum,** Copperfield Road, E3
Illustrates the life of poor of the East End in Victorian
London. Open: Wed. and Thurs.10 am to 5 pm. 1st Sunday
in the month 2-5 pm. *Station:* Mile End.

■ **Rangers House,** Chesterfield Walk, Greenwich, SE10
This fine 18th. century house with its remarkable long
gallery stands on the edge of Greenwich Park. It now
houses the Wernher Collection of paintings and treasures,
including medieval and Renaissance works of art.
Admission Charge. Open: Mon. Tues. Wed. & Sun. April to
end Sept. by guided tours only 11 a.m. and 2 p.m. *Station:*
see the National Maritime Museum.

■ **Richmond Park, Surrey.** ✪✪
An extensive Royal Park, first enclosed by Charles Ist. in
1637. This rolling landscape of forest trees and
undergrowth, roamed by herds of deer, is big enough to
get lost in. Isabella Plantation is a noted woodland garden.
Open daily. *Stations*: Richmond. D. or North Sheen or
Richmond, by train from Waterloo.

■ **Royal Air Force Museum,** Grahame Park Way, NW9.
✪✪ ✪ Portrays the dramatic history of military aviation
and aircraft from World War 1 onwards.
Battle of Britain Hall with its collection of fighter planes
vividly displays the events and those involved in the battle
for supremacy of the sky in 1940.
Bomber Hall tells the story of the development of aerial
bombing and displays many famous aircraft.
Milestones of Flight Hall illustrates the history of aviation
from airships to supersonic flight.
Open: 10 a.m. to 6 p.m. daily. Closed 24th - 26th
December. New Year's Day. *Station:* Colindale. N.

■ **Royal Artillery Museum,** see Firepower.

■ **Royal Naval College,** Greenwich, SE10 ✪
Stands on the site of the 15th. century Palace of Placentia,
birthplace of Henry VIII and his daughters Mary and
Elizabeth. Rebuilt by a succession of architects including
Wren, the palace became Greenwich Hospital in 1705;
(the naval equivalent of the Royal Hospital for soldiers at
Chelsea); and afterwards, in 1873, a college for the higher
education of Naval Officers and now houses the University
of Greenwich and Trinity College of Music.
The Discover Greenwich Visitor Centre, King William Walk,
SE10, the magnificent Chapel of 1789 by James 'Athenian'
Stuart and the unique Painted Hall by Sir James Thornhill
are all open to the public.

Open: normally 10 a.m. to 5 p.m. daily, subject to functions. Closed Christmas. *Admission Charge.*
Station: See the National Maritime Museum.

■ **Royal Observatory Greenwich,** Greenwich Park, SE10
✪✪✪✪ Part of the National Maritime Museum housed in apartments built in 1675 by Wren for the first astronomer Royal. New interactive astronomy galleries and state-of-the-art planetarium help explain some of the mysteries of the universe. Home of Greenwich Mean Time and the Meridian Line, where you can stand with one foot in the east and one in the west ! and see the time-ball fall at 1 o'clock precisely.
Open and Station: as the National Maritime Museum.
Planetarium shows daily. Admission charges.

■ **Syon House,** London Road, Brentford, Middlesex. ✪
The summer home of the Duke of Northumberland, Syon was originally a monastery built by Henry V in 1415. Much later a new house was built on the site incorporating parts of the monastery. The 16th century Italianate style exterior remains largely unaltered, the interior was redesigned by Robert Adam in the 1760s with typical plasterwork, pillars and statues. There are many paintings, including portraits by Reynolds and Gainsborough. Gardens laid out by Capability Brown.
Admission Charge. Open: House 11 a.m. to 5 p.m. Wed. Thurs. Sun. & Bank Holiday Mondays, end March to end Oct. Garden: Summer months daily 10.30 a.m. to 5 p.m.
Stations: Gunnersbury. D. then bus. Or Brentford by train from Waterloo.

■ **Thames Barrier,** Barrier Approach, SE7
Built to save London from flooding, the Barrier consists of huge movable steel gates pivoted between concrete piers; hydraulic machinery can lift the gates from the riverbed in 30 minutes. On the south side an exhibition, audio-visual presentation and viewing facilities are open for the public.
Admission Charge. Open: 10.30 am. to 5 pm Thursday to Sunday. Daily during School Holidays. *Station:* Charlton by train from Charing Cross or London Bridge.

■ **Thorpe Park,** Staines Road, Chertsey, Surrey ✪
Theme Park and fun fair with over 70 attractions around a lakeland setting; also working farm and craft shops.
Admission Charge. Open: times vary; closed winter months. *Station:* Staines by train from Waterloo, then bus.

■ **William Morris Gallery,** Lloyd Park, Forest Road, E17
Devoted to the life and work of William Morris, his followers and the Morris Company.
Open: 10 am. to 5 pm Wednesday to Sunday and Bank Holidays. *Station:* Walthamstow Central. V.

■ **Warner Bros. Studio Tour - The Making of Harry Potter,** Leavesden Studios, South Way, Watford
Behind the scenes tour of the most successful film series of all time, the sets, costume, animatronics, special effects. Tickets must be booked in advance via www.wbstudiotour.co.uk.

■ **Wimbledon Lawn Tennis Museum,** All England Tennis Club, Church Road, SW19.
The history of tennis, displays of trophies and features on tennis stars. *Admission Charge.* Open: 10 am. to 5.30 pm. daily, to 5 p.m. winter. Varies during The Championships. *Stations:* Southfields D. Wimbledon Park D.

■ **Windsor Castle,** Windsor, Berkshire. ✪✪✪
A royal residence since William the Conqueror first built a wood and earth castle here; this massive castle is now the largest in England and dominates the town skyline. When Her Majesty, Queen Elizabeth is here, the Royal Standard flies from the Round Tower. The State Apartments, rebuilt by Charles II, and richly furnished, contain many works of art by the Old Masters from the Royal Art Collection.
St. George's Chapel, a superb example of Perpendicular architecture, was begun for Edward IV as a private chapel for Knights of the Garter. Windsor Great Park with its famous Long Walk, and Virginia Water, once formed part of the ancient Royal Forest of Windsor.
Changing of the Guard takes place at 11am Mon. to Sat. in summer months, on alternate days winter months.
Admission Charge: Open: Castle and St George's Chapel, daily 9.45 a.m. to 5.15 p.m. (to 4.15 p.m. Nov. to Feb.). Notes: closed on certain days throughout the year for official or Royal functions, Semi-State Rooms are open winter months only, for details telephone 020 7766 7304. St. George's Chapel is closed to visitors on Sundays.
Stations: Windsor and Eton Central from Paddington, via Slough; or Windsor and Eton Riverside from Waterloo Main Line Stations.

■   **PAGEANTRY**

■ **CEREMONY OF THE KEYS**
Tower of London, continues after 700 years to be a 10 p.m. nightly event. The Chief Yeoman Warder—in scarlet coat, Tudor bonnet, and carrying a lantern—with foot Guard escort, locks up the several gates.
For admission write to: The Ceremony of the Keys, Waterloo Block, H.M. Tower of London, EC3N 4AB enclosing a stamped and addressed envelope.

■ **CHANGING OF THE GUARD** ✪✪✪ ✪

BUCKINGHAM PALACE. Takes place at 11.30 on a variable timetable of alternate days, or daily when possible during the Summer months. For up-to-date information telephone 020 7766 7300, see Visit London page 46 or the notice board at the Buckingham Palace gates.

The ceremony is carried out by one of the five regiments of Foot Guards, marching to the band, and resplendent in scarlet tunics and black bearskins (cancelled in very wet weather).

HORSE GUARDS Courtyard, Whitehall. Daily at 11 a.m. (Sundays, 10 a.m.) Ceremony by one of the two regiments of Household Cavalry either the Royal Horse Guard in blue tunics, or the Life Guards in scarlet. Traditional breastplates are worn by both regiments.

■ **LORD MAYOR'S SHOW**

A colourful annual procession (usually second Saturday November) when the newly-elected Lord Mayor drives in his gilded state coach, drawn by six horses to the Law Courts to take the oath.

■ **OPENING OF THE ROYAL COURTS OF JUSTICE**

The first Monday in October, all Her Majesty's Judges and members of the Bar—in State robes and full-bottomed wigs—attend a service in Westminster Abbey. Then, led by the Lord Chancellor, they walk in procession to the House of Lords; and after lunching there drive to the Law Courts. The first Motion of the year, taken in his court by the Lord Chancellor, constitutes the opening of all the courts.

■ **REMEMBRANCE SUNDAY**

Annually, on the Sunday nearest November 11th, the Queen, the Prime Minister, Ministers, and members of the Opposition, take up their places by the Cenotaph, for the 11 a.m. two minutes silence The Queen leads the laying of wreaths in memory of those killed in battle since 1914.

■ **STATE OPENING OF PARLIAMENT**

After each General Election, and also annually normally at the end October or early November.

The Queen wearing her crown and robes of state, and escorted by Life Guards and Royal Horse Guards, is driven in her state coach along the Mall and Whitehall to the Houses of Parliament. There, in the House of Lords, she makes her speech from the throne, to both the Lords and Members of Parliament, who will have been summoned from the House of Commons.

■ **TROOPING THE COLOUR** ✪✪✪

Every June, on the Saturday nearest to the Queen's official birthday. This ceremony—dating from 1750—takes place on the Horse Guards Parade. The Queen, accompanied by Household Cavalry, and Guardsmen, travels there from Buckingham Palace and back again, to the strains of martial music.

■ BRASS RUBBING

London Brass Rubbing Centre.
St. Martin in the Fields, St. Martin's Place. 2B 82
Open 10 a.m. to 6p.m. Monday to Wednesday. 10 am. to 8 pm Thursday to Saturday. 11.30 am. to 5 pm. Sunday.

■ VIEWPOINTS

For panoramic viewpoints visit the following

City Hall -4C86	St. Paul's Cathedral -5C72
Emirates Air Line -see p36	Shard, The -4A 86
Golden Jubilee Bridges -3D83	South Bank -3D83
	Tower Bridge Walkway -3D87
London Eye -5D83	
Millennium Bridge -2D85	Wellington Arch -5A80
Monument, The -1A86	Westminster Cathedral -3E93
Oxo Tower Wharf -2A84	

■ WALKS IN CENTRAL LONDON

Places in blue type appear in alphabetical order from page 2, together with description and admission times.

■ One day: Starting at Buckingham Palace a walk along Birdcage Walk brings you to Parliament Square, with Westminster Abbey, the Houses of Parliament and Big Ben. Leaving Westminster Bridge on the right; walk up Whitehall past Downing Street and the Horse Guards to Trafalgar Square, where are Nelson's Column and the National Gallery. If your interests are historical and architectural take a bus along the Strand past the Law Courts to Fleet Street and St. Paul's Cathedral, and from there a bus to the Monument. A walk along Eastcheap and Great Tower Street brings you to the Tower of London.

If you prefer to see the West End shopping centre, take a bus from Trafalgar Square through Piccadilly Circus to Regent Street, walk north up to Oxford Circus, then turn left- west along Oxford Street, down Bond Street, and then left again at Piccadilly, which will bring you back to Piccadilly Circus, passing Burlington Arcade.

■ Two days: Take the underground to Tower Hill and nearby is the Tower of London with Tower Bridge beyond. Across the river are seen H.M.S. Belfast and the spires of Southwark Cathedral.
A walk along Lower Thames Street and past Old Billingsgate Fish Market brings you to the Monument, from

which King William Street leads to the heart of the City, with the Bank of England, the Mansion House and the Royal Exchange among many other famous buildings. From here St. Paul's Cathedral is a short bus ride or walk. Almost any bus going down Ludgate Hill continues through what was once the newspaper centre of Fleet Street to the Strand. On the right are the Royal Courts of Justice, and in the middle of the road the island churches of St. Clement Danes and St. Mary-le-Strand.

The Strand opens into Trafalgar Square, with its fountains, Nelson's Column, Admiralty Arch and the National Gallery. Any bus down Whitehall passes the entrance to the Horse Guards where two mounted sentries are on guard. On the left is Inigo Jones's Banqueting House, from which Charles I was led to his execution. Government offices line Whitehall, and on the right is the famous Downing Street. The Cenotaph is slightly beyond and soon Whitehall opens out into Parliament Square.

Here, the Houses of Parliament, St. Margaret's Church and Westminster Abbey form an impressive group. Take a bus proceeding along Victoria Street—on the right is the New Scotland Yard building, on the left rises the Campanile of Westminster Cathedral—to Victoria Station, and walk along Buckingham Palace Road to Buckingham Palace; where the Royal Standard will be flying if Her Majesty the Queen is in residence. Walk along the tree-lined Mall and skirt the battlemented walls of St. James's Palace, Pall Mall, with its well-known clubs, is soon reached. Farther along Pall Mall is Waterloo Place, with the Duke of York's Column in the centre, and by turning left up Regent Street you come to Piccadilly Circus. A bus up Regent Street to Oxford Circus, and another along Oxford Street to Museum Street, brings you near to the British Museum. From here it is only a short distance to London University.

Three days: The same route should be followed, but more time devoted to the Tower of London, St. Paul's Cathedral, The National Gallery in Trafalgar Square, Westminster Abbey and the British Museum. Then take the Central Line underground from Tottenham Court Road to Queensway, and walk south along the Broad Walk through Kensington Gardens. On the right lies Kensington Palace, on the left the Round Pond. On reaching Kensington Road turn left to the Albert Memorial, the Royal Albert Hall and the museums: the Science Museum, the Natural History Museum, and the Victoria and Albert Museum. Close by is the Roman Catholic Brompton Oratory and the busy shopping centres of Brompton Road and Knightsbridge.

Four or more days: The Wallace Collection in Manchester Square should be visited; Hyde Park; Regent's Park with its London Zoo; also Lincoln's Inn and The Temple which retain their unique atmosphere of 'old London'.

TOURIST INFORMATION

■ **VISIT LONDON** www.visitlondon.com
London's tourist information service, where to go, things to do, transport, essential information, tours, shopping, sport, restaurants and accommodation.

■ **TOURIST INFORMATION CENTRES**
Information is also available at Travel Information Centres see page 47.
City of London Information Centre, St. Paul's Churchyard, 020-7332 1456 –5C 72 Open 9.30 am to 5.30 pm Mon to Sat 10 am to 4 pm Sun. Closed 25-26 Dec.
Greenwich Tourist Information Centre, Pepys House, 2 Cutty Sark Gardens, SE 10, 087 0608 2000.
Open daily 10 am to 5 pm. Closed 25-26 Dec.

■ **TOURIST DISCOUNT CARDS**
London Pass, combines admittance to over 60 visitor attractions, tours and cruises. The London Transport Travelcard is an optional extra.
Available from www.londonpass.com Tel: 020 7293 0972 and www.visitlondon.com

■ **RIVER THAMES BOAT TRIPS** ✪✪
FROM WESTMINSTER PIER **1C 94**   EMBANKMENT PIER **3D 83** and LONDON EYE PIER **5D 83**
Regular trips to Tower of London, Greenwich and Thames Barrier downstream: also services to Kew Gardens, Richmond and Hampton Court upstream.
FROM TOWER PIER **3C 86**
Regular trips to Greenwich and Thames Barrier downstream; also Westminster and the London Eye upstream.

■ **CANAL TRIPS** ✪
Jason's Trip, Little Venice, 2D 65 For bookings, www.jasons.co.uk
*Jenny Wren Canal Trips, Camden Lock, Camden High Street, NW1. For bookings telephone 020 7485 4433.
London Waterbus Company, Little Venice, 2D 65 and
* Camden Lock, Camden High Street, NW1
020 7482 2550

■ **ROUND LONDON SIGHTSEEING TOURS** ✪✪
Circular tours run from the designated bus stops at many central locations, (Piccadilly Circus, Trafalgar Square etc.). They tour a variety of routes around the main tourist areas, and provide a hop-on, hop-off service for visiting the

attractions on the route, spoken commentary, and usually open top buses.
Big Bus Company 020 7233 9533
Golden Tours 020 7630 2028
Original London Sightseeing Tour 020 8877 1722

■ **CONDUCTED COACH TOURS** ✪
Tours are guide conducted in luxury coaches to some of the famous show places in and around London. All seats bookable. For information and to reserve seats apply to a Tourist or Travel Information Centre, Victoria Coach Station or travel agents.

* Outside Central London area mapped.

TRANSPORT INFORMATION

■ **BUSES AND UNDERGROUND RAILWAY**
For enquiries on buses, underground trains and Docklands Light Railway services.
24 hour travel information Tel: 0343 222 1234.
www.tfl.gov.uk

■ **TRAVEL INFORMATION CENTRES**
At Piccadilly Circus 2E 81, King's Cross St. Pancras 3B 62 and Liverpool Street 3B 74 Underground Stations.
Also Euston 3E 61, Paddington 4F 65 and Victoria 3C 92 Main Line Railway Stations, Victoria Coach Station 5B 92, Gatwick Airport (North Terminal) and Heathrow Airport Terminals 1,2,3 Underground Station.

■ **TRAVELCARD and OYSTER CARD**
On sale at Underground Stations, Transport for London Travel Information Centres and Main Line Railway Stations. Travelcards give access to London Buses, Underground Trains and Tramlink, also the Docklands Light Railway and most parts of the Rail system within Greater London.
    Travelcards are good value, save time as well as the need to buy separate tickets for each journey. Travelcards can be bought for 1 day, 3 days or 7 days (photograph required for 7 days). They cannot be used on coach tours.
    Oyster Card (deposit required) is an alternative that enables you to pre-pay for your journeys at reduced rates.

■ **DOCKLANDS LIGHT RAILWAY**
Enquiries 0343 222 1234.
From Bank Station 5F 73 or Tower Gateway Station 1E 87 Lewisham Line for Canary Wharf, Cutty Sark and Greenwich. Woolwich Arsenal Line for London City Airport. Beckton Line for ExCeL.

■ **TAXIS**
Scale of charges is shown in each taxi-cab.

■ **COACHES**
Coaches travel from London to most Towns and Cities, seats must be booked in advance.
Victoria Coach Station, 164 Buckingham Palace Road. 5B 92. Open daily 7 am to 10 pm.
National Express Coach Service information
Tel: 08717 81 81 81 for advice, ticket ammendments, refunds and cancellations.

■ **GREEN LINE COACHES**
Connecting Central London with towns in the surrounding counties. Green Line Coach Station, Bulleid Way, Eccleston Bridge. Tel: 0844 801 7261. 4C 92

■ **MAIN LINE RAILWAY TERMINI**
Note: Through tickets for any station, irrespective of region, may be obtained from any station booking office. Seats and sleeping berths may be reserved in the same way.

■ NATIONAL RAIL ENQUIRIES 24 hours. daily
Tel. 08457 48 49 50

Blackfriars 1B 84. Cannon Street 1F 85. Charing Cross 3C 82. Euston 3E 61. Fenchurch Street 1C 86. King's Cross 2B 62. Liverpool Street 3B 74. London Bridge 4A 86. Marylebone 1C 66. Paddington 4F 65. St. Pancras International 2B 62. Victoria 4C 92. Waterloo 5F 83.

■ **EUROSTAR**
Through services direct to Paris and Brussels via the Channel Tunnel.
Information and Bookings Telephone 08432 186186.
St. Pancras International Station 2B 62.

■ **AIRPORTS**
Gatwick, Gatwick, West Sussex. 0344 892 0322
Heathrow, Hounslow, Middlesex. 0844 335 1801
London City, Silvertown, E16 020 7646 0088
Luton, Luton, Bedfordshire. 01582 405100
Stansted, Stansted, Essex. 0844 335 1803

■ **AIRPORT LINKS**
■ **Gatwick-Central London**
1. Gatwick Express, from Victoria Station.
2. National Express Coach, from Victoria Coach Station.

■ **Heathrow-Central London**
1. Heathrow Express, from Paddington Station.
2. Heathrow Connect, from Paddington Station.
3. Underground Train, Piccadilly Line fron central London.
4. National Express Coach from Victoria Coach Station.

■ **London City-Cental London**
   Docklands Light Railway from Bank or Tower Gateway.

■ **Luton-Central London**
  1. Rail services from either St. Pancras International Station, Farringdon, City Thameslink or Blackfriars Stations to Luton Airport Parkway for connecting Shuttlebus service.
  2. Greenline Coach 757 from Buckingham Palace Road, beside Victoria Station.

■ **Stansted-Central London**
  1. Stansted Express from Liverpool Street Station.
  2. National Express Coach service from Victoria Coach Station.

■ **Heathrow-Gatwick-Stansted**
  National Express Coach airport transfer service.

■ **LOST PROPERTY**
  Property lost on Buses, London Underground, London Overground and black taxi cabs is forwarded to —

  Tfl Lost Property Office, 200 Baker Street, NW1 5RZ –1E 67. Open 8.30 a.m. - 4 p.m. Monday to Friday, closed Bank Holidays. 0343 222 1234.

  Property lost on boats, trams and minicabs is held by the operator.

PLACES OF WORSHIP

■ **BAPTIST**
  Bloomsbury Central Church, Shaftesbury Avenue. 4B 70 *Station:* Tottenham Court Road
  Gower Street Memorial Chapel, Shaftesbury Avenue. 5B 70 *Station:* Tottenham Court Road
  Metropolitan Tabernacle, Elephant & Castle 4C 96 *Station:* Elephant & Castle
  Westminster, Horseferry Road 3A 94 *Station:* St. James's Park

■ **CHRISTIAN SCIENCE**
  Second Church of Christ, Scientist, 104 Palace Gardens Terrace, W8 3A 76 *Station:* Notting Hill Gate

■ **CHURCH OF ENGLAND**
  All Saints, Margaret Street. 4D 69
  Station: Oxford Circus
  All Souls, Langham Place. 3C 68
  Station: Oxford Circus
  Chapel Royal, St. James's Palace. 4E 81
  Station: Green Park
  Christ Church Spitalfields, Commercial Street. 2D 75
  Station: Aldgate East
  St. George (Hanover Square), St. George Street. 1C 80
  Station: Oxford Circus
  St Giles-in-the-Fields, St. Giles High Street. 4A 70

Station: Tottenham Court Road
St James's, Piccadilly. 2E 81
Station: Piccadilly Circus
St Margaret's, Westminster. 1B 94
Station: Westminster
St. Martin-in-the- Fields, St. Martin's Place. 2B 82
Station: Charing Cross
St. Marylebone, Marylebone Road. 1A 68
Station: Baker Street
St. Paul's, Covent Garden. 1C 82
Station: Covent Garden
St. Paul's Cathedral, Ludgate Hill. 5C 72
Station: St Paul 's
Southwark Cathedral, Cathedral Street. 3F 85
Station: London Bridge
Westminster Abbey, Parliament Square. 2B 94
Station: Westminster

■ **CHURCH OF SCOTLAND**
Crown Court Church, Russell Street. 5C 70
Station: Holborn
St. Columba's, Pont Street. 3D 91
Stations: Knightsbridge, Sloane Square

■ **DANISH CHURCH**
Danish Church, Regent's Park. 2B 60
Station: Regent's Park

■ **DUTCH CHURCH**
Dutch Church, Austin Friars. 4A 74   *Station:* Bank

■ **FRENCH PROTESTANT**
Eglise Protestante, Française de Londres,
9 Soho Square. 4F 69
Station: Tottenham Court Road

■ **GREEK ORTHODOX**
St. Sophia's, Moscow Road. 1B 76   *Station:* Bayswater

■ **INDEPENDENT EVANGELICAL**
Westminster Chapel, Buckingham Gate. 2E 93
Station: St James's Park

■ **INTERDENOMINATIONAL**
American Church in London, 79 Tottenham Court Road,
2E 69   *Station:* Goodge Street

■ **JEWISH**
Bevis Marks Synagogue, 4C 74   *Station:* Aldgate
Central Synagogue, Gt. Portland Street. 2C 68
Station: Gt. Portland Street
New West End Synagogue, 10 St. Petersburgh Place
2B 76   *Station:* Queensway
*Spanish and Portuguese Synagogue, St James's Gardens,
W11   *Station:* Holland Park

West London Synagogue (Reform), 34 Upper Berkeley Street. 5D 67   *Station:* Marble Arch

■ **LUTHERAN**
St. Anne & St Agnes (Lutheran) Church, Gresham Street. 4D 73   *Station:* St. Paul's

■ **METHODIST**
Central Hall, Tothill Street, Westminster 1A 94
Stations: Westminster, St. James's Park
Chiltern Street Welsh Methodist, Chiltern Street 2F 67   *Station:* Baker Street.
(Last Sunday in month 6.30 pm only)
Hinde Street Church, Theyer Street. 4A 68
Station: Bond Street
Wesley's Chapel, City Road. 1A 74
Stations: Moorgate, Old Street.

■ **MOSLEM**
London Central Mosque, Regent's Park. 4C 58
Station: Baker Street

■ **ROMAN CATHOLIC**
Church of the Immaculate Conception, Farm Street, Berkeley Square. 2B 80
Stations: Green Park, Bond Street
French Catholic Church of Notre Dame de France, Leicester Place, off Leicester Square. 1A 82
Station: Leicester Square
Oratory, The, Brompton Road. 3B 90
Station: South Kensington
St. George's Cathedral, St. George's Road. 2A 96
Station: Lambeth North
St. James's, Spanish Place, Manchester Square. 3A 68
Station: Bond Street
St Patrick Catholic Church, 21 Soho Square.
5A 70   *Station:* Tottenham Court Road
Ukranian Catholic Cathedral, Duke Street. 1A 80
Station: Bond Street
Westminster Cathedral, Ashley Place. 3D 93
Station: Victoria

■ **RUSSIAN ORTHODOX CHURCH IN EXILE**
All Saints Cathedral, Ennismore Gardens, SW7.
1B 90   *Station:* South Kensington

■ **SALVATION ARMY**
Regent Hall, 275 Oxford Street. 5C 68
Station: Oxford Circus

■ **SOCIETY OF FRIENDS (QUAKERS)**
Friends House, Euston Road. 5F 61
Station: Euston Square
Toynbee Hall, 28 Commercial Street. 3E 75

Station: Aldgate East
Westminster Meeting House, 52 St. Martin's Lane. 1B 82
Station: Leceister Square

■ **SWEDISH**
Swedish Church, 11 Harcourt Street. 3C 66
Stations: Edgware Road, Marylebone

■ **SWISS CHURCH**
Eglise Suisse de Londres, 79 Endell Street. 4B 70
Station: Tottenham Court Road

■ **UNITARIAN**
Essex Church, Palace Gardens Terrace. 3A 76
Station: Notting Hill Gate

■ **UNITED REFORMED**
Christ Church and Upton Chapel, Westminster Bridge
Road. 2F 95   *Station:* Lambeth North
City Temple, Holborn Viaduct. 3A 72 *Station:* St. Paul's
Lumen URC, Regent Square. 4C 62
Stations: King's Cross, St. Pancras

■ **WELSH**
Welsh Baptist Chapel, 30 Eastcastle Street. 4E 69
Station: Oxford Circus.

*Outside Central London area mapped.

■ ░░░░░░░░░░░░░░░░ **TICKETS** ░░░░░░░░░░░░░░░░

Tickets should be bought from either the venue or a
reputable ticket agency.   Popular shows are often sold out
weeks or months ahead, it is however possible to queue for
'returns'- returned tickets on the night of performance;
these are available only from the venue box office.

■ The **Half Price Ticket Booth** can also offer tickets on the
day of performance.   Beware of ticket touts who may
approach you in such queues.
Half Price Ticket Booth, Leicester Square 2A 82
(open to Personal callers only).

■ **Theatre, Concert, Events and Sports Ticket Agencies:**
Keith Prowse: www.keithprowse.com
Stargreen: www.stargreen.com
Ticketmaster: www.ticketmaster.co.uk

■ ░░░░░░░░░░░░░░ **WEST END CINEMAS** ░░░░░░░░░░░░░░

Nearest station shown in italics.
Barbican, Beech Street. 2E 73 *Barbican, Moorgate*
Barbican Centre, Silk Street. 2E 73 *Barbican, Moorgate*
BFI Southbank, South Bank. 3E 83 *Waterloo*
Cine Lumiere, Queensberry Place   4F 89
      South Kensington
*Cineworld Chesea, 279 Kings Road. SW3 *Sloane Square*

*Cineworld Fulham Road, SW10 *South Kensington*
Cineworld Haymarket, Haymarket. 2F 81 *Piccadilly Circus*
Curzon Bloomsbury, Brunswick Square. 5C 62 *Russell
    Square*
*Curzon Chelsea, 206 King's Road. SW3. *Sloane Square*.
Curzon Mayfair, Curzon Street. 4B 80 *Green Park*
Curzon Soho, Shaftesbury Avenue. 5A 70
    Piccadilly Circus
Curzon Victoria, Victoria Street. 2E 93 *Victoria*
Empire, Leicester Square. 1A 82 *Leicester Square*
Everyman Baker Street, Baker Street. 2F 67 *Baker Street.*
ICA Nash House, The Mall. 3A 82 *Charing Cross*
IMAX BFI Imax, Waterloo. 4F 83 *Waterloo*
Odeon Covent Garden, Shaftesbury Avenue. 5A 70
    Leicester Square
Odeon Leicester Square, 2A 82 *Leicester Square*
Odeon Marble Arch, Marble Arch. 5E 67 *Marble Arch*
Odeon Panton Street, Panton Street. 2A 82
    Piccadilly Circus
Odeon Studios, see Odeon Leicester Square
Odeon Tottenham Court Road, Tottenham Court
    Road. 3F 69 *Tottenham Court Road*
Odeon, Whiteleys Centre, Queensway. 5C 64 *Queensway*
Picturehouse Central, Shaftesbury Avenue. 1F 81
    Piccadilly Circus
Prince Charles, Leicester Place, off Leicester Square.
    1A 82 *Leicester Square*
Regent Street, 309 Regent Street 4C68, *Oxford Circus*
*Screen on the Green, Islington Green, N1. *Angel*
Vue Piccadilly (Apollo), Regent Street. 2F 81 *Piccadilly
    Circus*
Vue West End, Leicester Square. 1A 82 *Leicester Square*

*Outside Central London area mapped.

Nearest station shown in italics.
Adelphi, Strand. 2C 82 *Charing Cross*
Aldwych, Aldwych. 1D 83 *Covent Garden*
Ambassadors, West Street. 5B 70 *Leicester Square*
Apollo, Shaftesbury Avenue. 1F 81 *Piccadilly Circus*
Apollo Victoria, Wilton Road. 3D 93 *Victoria*
Arts, 6 Great Newport Street. 1B 82 *Leicester Square*
Barbican, Silk Street. 2E 73 *Barbican, Moorgate*
Bloomsbury, Gordon Street. 5F 61. *Euston Square*
Bridewell, St Bride Foundation, Bride La. 11 Ca *Blackfriars*
Britten Opera Theatre, Royal College of Music,
    Prince Consort Road. 2F 89 *South Kensington*
Cambridge, Earlham Street. 5B 70 *Leicester Square*
Charing Cross, The Arches, off Villiers Street. 3C 82
    Charing Cross, Embankment

53

Cockpit, Gateforth Street. 1B 66 *Marylebone*
Coliseum, St. Martin's Lane. 2B 82 *Leicester Square*
Criterion, Piccadilly. 2F 81 *Piccadilly Circus*
Dominion, Tottenham Court Rd. 4A 70 *Tottenham Ct. Rd*
Donmar Warehouse, Earlham Street. 5B 70
    Leicester Square
Dorfman, See National
Drury Lane, Catherine Street. 5D 71 *Covent Garden*
Duchess, Catherine Street. 1D 83 *Covent Garden*
Duke of York's, St. Martin's Lane. 2B 82
    Leicester Square
English National Opera, see Coliseum
*Eventim, Queen Caroline Street, W6. *Hammersmith*
Fortune, Russell Street. 5C 70 *Covent Garden*
Garrick, Charing Cross Road. 2B 82 *Leicester Square*
Gielgud, Shaftesbury Avenue. 1F 81 *Piccadilly Circus*
Globe, See Shakespeare's Globe
Greenwood, Weston Street. 5A 86 *London Bridge*
*Hackney Empire, 291 Mare Street. E8
    Hackney Central
Harold Pinter, Panton Street. 2A 82 *Piccadilly Circus*
Haymarket, Haymarket. 2A 82 *Piccadilly Circus*
Her Majesty's, Haymarket. 3F 81 *Piccadilly Circus*
ICA Carlton House Terrace 3A 82 *Charing Cross*
Jermyn Street, Jermyn Street. 2E 81 *Piccadilly Circus*
Leicester Square, Leicester Place, Leicester Square.
    IA 82 *Leicester Square*
Lyceum, Wellington Street. ID 83 *Charing Cross*
Lyric, Shaftesbury Avenue. 1F 81 *Piccadilly Circus*
*Lyric Hammersmith, King Street. W6 *Hammersmith*
Lyttelton, See National
Menier, Southwark Street, 4E 85 *London Bridge*
National, Upper Ground, South Bank. 3E 83 *Waterloo*
New Diorama, 15-16 Triton Street. 5D 61 *Gt. Portland St.*
New London, Drury Lane. 4C 71 *Covent Garden*
Noel Coward, St. Martins Lane. 1B 82 *Leicester Square*
Novello, Aldwych. 1D 83 *Covent Garden*
Old Vic, Waterloo Road. 5A 84 *Waterloo*
Olivier, See National
Open Air, Regent's Park. 4F 59 *Baker Street.*
Palace, Shaftesbury Avenue. 1F 70 *Leicester Square*
Palladium, Argyll Street. 5D 69 *Oxford Circus*
Place, The, Duke's Road.. 4A 62 *Euston*
Peacock, Portugal Street. 5D 71 *Holborn*
Phoenix, Charing Cross Road. 5A 70 *Tottenham Court Rd.*
Piccadilly, Denman Street. 1E 81 *Piccadilly Circus*
Playhouse, Northumberland Avenue, 3C 82
    Charing Cross
Prince Edward, Old Compton Street 5F 69
    Leicester Square
Prince of Wales, Coventry Street. 2F 81 *Piccadilly Circus*

Queen's, Shaftesbury Avenue. 1F 81 *Piccadilly Circus*
Rambert, Upper Ground. 14 Aa *Waterloo*
Robin Howard Dance Theatre, Duke's Road.
   4A 62 *Euston*
Royal Court, Sloane Square. 5F 91
Royal National Theatre, See National
Royal Opera House, Covent Garden. 5C 70 *Covent*
   Garden
*Sadler's Wells, Rosebery Avenue. EC1 *Angel*
St. James, Palace Street. 2D 93 *Victoria*
St. Martin's, West Street. 1B 82 *Leicester Square*
Sam Wanamaker, See Shakespeare's Globe
Savoy, Strand. 2D 83 *Embankment*
Shaftesbury, Shaftesbury Avenue. 4B 70
   Tottenham Court Road
Shakespears's Globe, Bankside. 3D 85 *London Bridge*
Shaw, Euston Road. 3A 62 *Euston*
Siobhan Davis Dance Centre, St. George's Road.
   3B 96 *Elephant & Castle*
Soho Theatre and Writers Centre, Dean St. 5F 69
   Oxford Circus
Theatre Royal Drury Lane, see Drury Lane
Theatre Royal Haymarket, see Haymarket
*Theate Royal Stratford East, Gerry Raffles
   Square. E15 *Stratford*
Trafalgar Studios, Whitehall. 3B 82 *Charing Cross*
Unicorn, Tooley Street, 4C 86 *London Bridge*
Union, Union Street. 4C 84 *Southwark*
Vanburgh, RADA, Malet Street. 1A 70 *Goodge Street*
Vaudeville, Strand. 2C 82 *Embankment*
Victoria Palace, Victoria Street. 3C 92 *Victoria*
Waterloo East, Brad Street, 4A 84 *Southwark*
Wilton's Music Hall, Grace's Alley, 1F 87 *Tower Hill*
Wyndham's, Charing Cross Road.1B 82 *Leicester Square*
Young Vic, The Cut. 5A 84 *Waterloo*

* Outside Central London area mapped.

CONCERT HALLS

Nearest station shown in italics.

Barbican Hall, Silk Street. 2E 73 *Barbican, Moorgate*
Cadogan Hall, Sloane Terrace 4F 91 *Sloane Square*
Central Hall, Tothill Street. 1A 94 *St. James's Park*
Conway Hall, Red Lion Square. 2D 71 *Holborn*
Guildhall School of Music and Drama, Barbican.
   2E 73 *Barbican, Moorgate*
Kings Place, York Way. 1C 62 *King's Cross St Pancras*
Logan Hall, Institute of Education, 20 Bedford Way.
   1A 70 *Russell Square*
*LSO St. Lukes, Old Street, EC1 *Old Street*
Purcell Room, South Bank. 3E 83 *Waterloo*

Queen Elizabeth Hall, South Bank. 3E 83 *Waterloo*
Royal Albert Hall, Kensington Gore. 1F 89
 South Kensington
Royal College of Music, Prince Consort Road.
 2F 89 *South Kensington*
Royal Festival Hall, Belvedere Road, South Bank.
 4E 83 *Waterloo*
St. John's Smth Square, Smith Square. 3B 94 *Westminster*
Scala, 275 Pentonville Road, 3C 62
 King's Cross St Pancras
*The O2 Arena, Peninsular Square, SE10.
 North Greenwich
*Wembley Arena, Empire Way, Wembley.
 Wembley Park
Wigmore Hall, 36 Wigmore Street. *4B 68 Bond Street.*
 Oxford Circus

* Outside Central London area mapped.

SELECTED SHOPS

Debenhams – 5B 68
Fenwick – 1C 80
Fortnum and Mason – 3E 81
Foyle's – 5A 70
Habitat – 1D 81 / 2F 69
Hamleys –1D 81
Harrods – 2D 91
Harvey Nichols – 1E 91
Heals – 2F 69
House of Fraser –5B 68
House of Fraser Victoria –
 3E 93
John Lewis – 5C 68
Liberty – 5D 69
London Silver Vaults –3F 71
Mappin and Webb – 1E 81
Marks and Spencer
 (Marble Arch) – 5F 67
Marks and Spencer
 (Oxford Circus) – 5D 69
Peter Jones – 5E 91
St.Christopher's Place– 4A68
Selfridges – 5A 68
Thomas Neal's –5B70
Top Shop – 4D69
Whiteleys Centre – 5B 64

GOVERNMENT OFFICES

Business, Innovation
 & Skills, Dept of – 2A94
Commonwealth Office –
 5B 82
Defence, Ministry of – 4C 82
Education
 Department of – 2A 94
Environment, Food & Rural
 Affairs, (Defra)
 Department of – 3B 94
Foreign Office – 5B 82
Home Office – 3A 94
Houses of Parliament –
 1C 94
Land Registry – 4E 71
Passport Office – 4C 92
Scotland Office – 5B 82
Transport
 Department of – 4A 94
Treasury – 5B 82
Wales Office –5B 82

AUCTIONEERS

Bonhams – 5B 68 & 2C 90
Christies – 3E 81 & 5F 89
Sotheby's – 1C 80
Spink – 2B 70

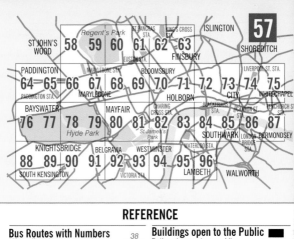

Map grid references:

ST JOHN'S WOOD · Regent's Park · ST PANCRAS STA. · KING'S CROSS STA. · ISLINGTON · SHOREDITCH

58 59 60 61 62 63 · FINSBURY

EUSTON STA.

PADDINGTON · MARYLEBONE STA. · BLOOMSBURY · LIVERPOOL ST. STA.

64 65 66 67 68 69 70 71 72 73 74 75

PADDINGTON STA. · MARYLEBONE · HOLBORN · CITY · WHITECHAPEL · FENCHURCH ST STA.

BAYSWATER · MAYFAIR · CHARING CROSS STA. · BLACKFRIARS STA. · CANNON ST.

76 77 78 79 80 81 82 83 84 85 86 87

Hyde Park · St James's Park · SOUTHWARK · LONDON BRIDGE STA. · BERMONDSEY

KNIGHTSBRIDGE · BELGRAVIA · WESTMINSTER · WATERLOO STA.

88 89 90 91 92 93 94 95 96

SOUTH KENSINGTON · VICTORIA STA. · LAMBETH · WALWORTH

REFERENCE

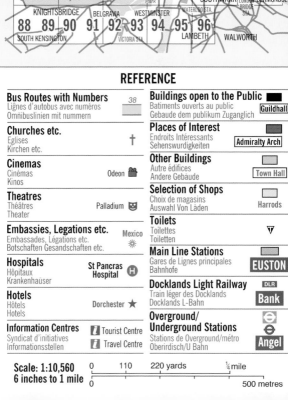

Bus Routes with Numbers
Lignes d'autobus avec numéros
Omnibuslinien mit nummern — 38

Churches etc.
Eglises
Kirchen etc. — †

Cinemas
Cinémas
Kinos — Odeon 🎬

Theatres
Théâtres
Theater — Palladium 🎭

Embassies, Legations etc.
Embassades, Légations etc.
Botschaften Gesandschaften etc. — Mexico ※

Hospitals
Hôpitaux
Krankenhaüser — St Pancras Hospital H

Hotels
Hôtels
Hotels — Dorchester ★

Information Centres
Syndicat d'initiatives
Informationsstellen — i Tourist Centre · i Travel Centre

Buildings open to the Public
Batiments ouverts au public
Gebaude dem publikum Zuganglich — Guildhall

Places of Interest
Endroits Intéressants
Sehenswurdigkeiten — Admiralty Arch

Other Buildings
Autre édifices
Andere Gebaude — Town Hall

Selection of Shops
Choix de magasins
Auswahl Von Läden — Harrods

Toilets
Toilettes
Toiletten — ▽

Main Line Stations
Gares de Lignes principales
Bahnhofe — EUSTON

Docklands Light Railway
Train léger des Docklands
Docklands L-Bahn — DLR Bank

Overground/Underground Stations
Stations de Overground/métro
Oberirdisch/U Bahn — Angel

Scale: 1:10,560
6 inches to 1 mile

0 — 110 — 220 yards — ¼ mile
0 — 500 metres

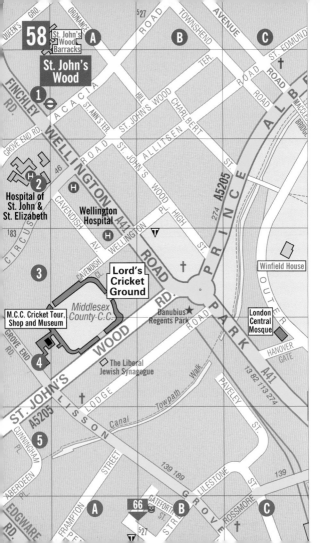

58

St. John's Wood Barracks

St. John's Wood

A **B** **C**

QUEEN'S GRO.
ORDNANCE
527 ROAD
TOWNSHEND AVENUE
ST. EDMUND'S
FINCHLEY RD.
GROVE END RD.
WELLINGTON ROAD A41
ACACIA ROAD
ST. ANN'S TER.
ST. JOHN'S WOOD
HILL
CHARLBERT
TER.
ROAD
ROAD
MACCLES BRIDGE

1

Hospital of St. John & St. Elizabeth
H
2
46
H
Wellington Hospital
CAVENDISH
ALLITSEN
ST. JOHN'S WOOD PL.
HIGH ST.
WOOD
A5205
274
PRINCE

CIRCUS
183
CAVENDISH AV.
H
WELLINGTON
ROAD
Winfield House

3
CAVENDISH CL.
Lord's Cricket Ground
RD.
PARK
OUTER

Middlesex County-C.C.
Danubius ★
Regents Park
London Central Mosque

M.C.C. Cricket Tour, Shop and Museum
GROVE END RD.
4
WOOD
Walk
HANOVER GATE
13 82 113 274
A41

□ The Liberal Jewish Synagogue
LODGE
PAVELEY
ST.

ST. JOHN'S
A5205
LISSON
Towpath
Canal
Walk
STREET

CUNNINGHAM PL.
5
139 189
GROVE
LILESTONE ST.
139
CROSSMORE

ABERDEEN PL.
EDGWARE RD.
FRAMPTON
A
66
GATEFORTH ST.
ST. R.
B
527
C

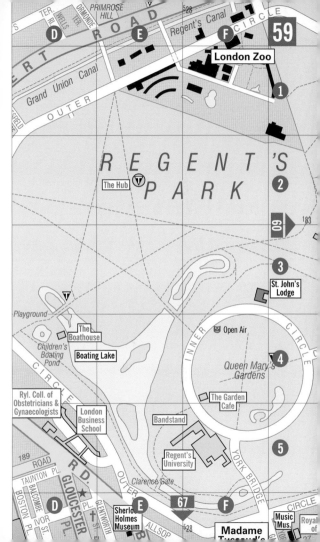

A **B** ★ York & Albany **C**

PRINCE ALBERT ROAD
PARK-WAY
DELANCY ST.
ARLINGTON
529
274

London Zoo

1

OUTER
GLOUCESTER GATE
ALBANY STREET
PARK
MORNINGTON
VILLAGE
MORNINGTON
ALBERT
MOR
C2

Danish Church †
Regent's Park Barracks

2

R E G E N T ' S

EAST
AUGUSTUS

CIRCLE
A4201
REDHILL ST.

183 **59**
Refreshments

P A R K

3

St. John's Lodge

Cumberland Gate
CUMBERLD. PL.
CHESTER
TER.

Regent's † Park

CUMBERLAN
MARKET

4

INNER
Open Air
CIRCLE CHESTER ROAD
▽
Queen Mary's Gardens
▽

Chester Gate
CHESTER GATE
C2

ROBERT

STREET

Westmins
Kingsway Co

e Garden Cafe

5

INNER
YORK BRIDGE

Playground

Royal College of Physicians

LONGFORD
OSNABURGH
†
Meliá
White Ho. ★
OSNABURGH TER.
Nev
Diora

CIRCLE
OUTER
GA.
YORK

A
Music Mus.
Royal Academy of Music
27

68
PARK CRESCENT
30

B
Regent's Park

EAST SQ.

CR.
Royal National

Great Portla
Street
H
529
▽

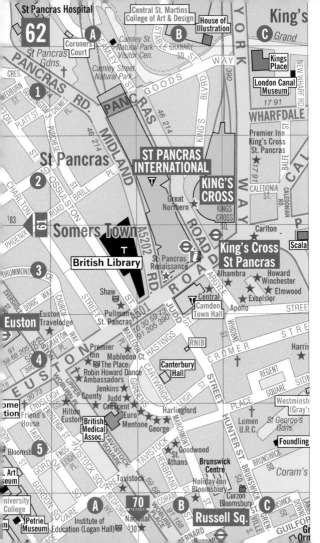

St Pancras Hospital

62

Central St. Martins
College of Art & Design

House of
Illustration

King's

A

Coroners
Court

St Pancras
Gdns.

Camley St.
Natural Park
Visitor Cen.

B

STABLE
GRANARY
SQ.

YORK WAY

C

Grand

Kings
Place

London Canal
Museum

NEW WHARF RD.

PANCRAS RD.
CRES.

WEDBURN ST.

ROSSINGTON ST.

1

ST.

CHENIES

PLATT ST.

PURCHESE ST.

CAMLEY ST.

Camley Street
Natural Park

MIDLAND   PANCRAS   RD.

GOODS

KING'S

BLVRD

390

WAY

46 214

WHARFDALE

Premier Inn
King's Cross
St. Pancras

CALEDONIA

CHARLTON

OSSULSTON

St Pancras

2

BRILL

ROAD

EUSTON

ST PANCRAS
INTERNATIONAL

KING'S
CROSS

Great
Northern

KINGS
CROSS
SQ.

ROAD

KING'S

CALEDONIAN RD.

CALEDONIA
ST.

P

183

PHOENIX

61

Somers Town

STREET

ROAD

British Library

St Pancras
Renaissance

Carlton

ROAD

King's Cross
St Pancras

Scala

3

DRUMMOND

CR

DORIC WAY

CHURCH

Shaw

A5202

A501

JUDD

Central
Camden
Town Hall

Alhambra

Argyle

Howard
Winchester

Elmwood

Excelsior

STREET

Euston
Travelodge

Pullman
St. Pancras

ST.

STREET

Apollo

Euston

4

EVERSHOLT

GRAFTON
PL.

UPPER   WOBURN   PL.

Premier
Inn

The Place
Robin Howard Dance

Ambassadors

Jenkins

County

Judd

Crescent

MABLEDON

HASTINGS

CARTWRIGHT

GARDENS

ST.

RNIB

Canterbury
Hall

LEIGH

CROMER

WHIDBORNE

STREE

Harris

REGENT

SQUARE

SIDM

5

EUSTON

ome
tion

Friend's
House

Bloomsbury

Hilton
Euston

British
Medical
Assoc.

ENDSLEIGH PL.

GORDON

LEIGH

ST.

TAVISTOCK SQUARE

Euro

Mentone George

Harlingford

MARCHMONT

HUNTER ST.

PLACE

Lumen
U.R.C.

St George's
Gdns.

Westminster
(Gray's)

Foundling

Art
seum

university
College

Petrie
Museum

GORDON SQUARE

ENDSLEIGH GARDENS

BEDFORD

WOBURN PLACE

TAVISTOCK SQUARE

A

Institute of
Education (Logan Hall)

70

National

Tavistock

St.
Athans

Goodwood

Brunswick
Centre

Holiday Inn
Bloomsbury

HERBRAND

CORAM

B

Russell Sq.

Brunswick

Curzon
Bloomsbury

Coram's

BRUNSWICK SQ.

MARCHMONT ST.

GRENVILLE

C

SWICK
SQ.

ORN

GUILFOR

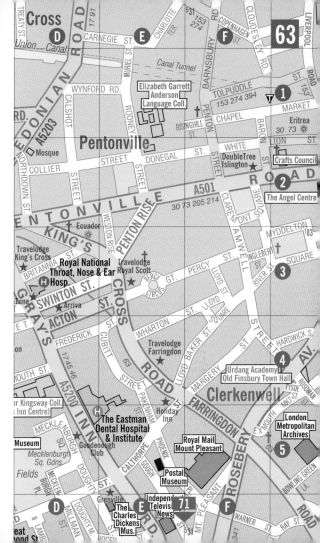

Cross

TREATY ST.
Union Canal

D

CARNEGIE ST.

E

CHARLOTTE TER.

531 753 274

COPENHAGEN

F

CLOUDESLEY RD.

LIVERPOOL

63

MURIEL ST.

Canal Tunnel

BARNSBURY RD.

ST.

RD.

WYNFORD RD.

CALSHOT ST.

A5203

RODNEY ST.

Elizabeth Garrett Anderson Language Coll.

TOLPUDDLE ST.
153 274 394

ROAD

MARKET

1

RISINGHILL ST.

CHAPEL

BARON ST.

Eritrea
30 73 ☀

NORTHDOWN ST.

Mosque

Pentonville

DONEGAL ST.

WHITE

LION ST.

DoubleTree Islington ★

Crafts Council

COLLIER

STREET

STREET

STREET

R O A D

2

PENTONVILLE

A501
30 73 205 214

CLAREMONT

The Angel Centre

KING'S

Ecuador ✝

WESTON RISE

PENTON RISE

AMWELL

MYDDELTON ✝

INGLEBERT ST.

'83

ENTONVILLE

SQUARE

Travelodge King's Cross

BRITANNIA ST.

Royal National Throat, Nose & Ear Hosp. **H**

Travelodge Royal Scott

PERCY CIRCUS

PERCY ST.

GT. PERCY ST.

LLOYD ST.

RIVER ST.

3

Tune

GRAY'S

SWINTON ST.

Arriva ★

CROSS

WHARTON

ST.

ST.

LLOYD BAKER ST.

LLOYD SQUARE

LLOYD ST.

STREET

HARDWICK S.

AV.

4

ACTON ST.

FREDERICK

CUBITT ST.

ST.

Travelodge Farringdon

MARGERY ST.

Urdang Academy Old Finsbury Town Hall

TYSOE ST.

ROSOMAN

MOUTH ST.

1 7 45 46

A5200 INN

STREET

PAKENHAM

ROAD

LLOYD BAKER ST.

63

Clerkenwell

FARRINGDON

EX'MOUTH

MKT.

London Metropolitan Archives

5

er Kingsway Coll. Inn Centre)

MECKLENBURGH

H

Holiday Inn

PHOENIX

Royal Mail Mount Pleasant

ROSEBERY

BOWLING GREEN LA.

Museum

SQ.

The Eastman Dental Hospital & Institute

Goodenough Club

CALTHORPE

GOUGH

Postal Museum

ROAD

Mecklenburgh Sq. Gdns.

MECKLEN. BURGH PL.

DOUGHTY

Grenville

ST.

Independent Television News

WARNER

Fields

D

MILLMAN

Great mond R.

DOUGHTY M.

LAMB.

E

The Charles Dickens Mus.

531

71

MT. PLEASANT

F

341

ST. RAY. ST.

ROAD

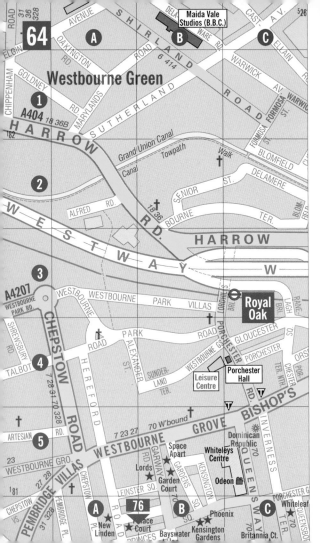

64

Westbourne Green

Maida Vale Studios (B.B.C.)

ROAD 31 36 328

AVENUE

SHIRLAND

A.V.

526

CAST.

ELGIN

OAKINGTON RD.

ROAD

DELA

WARE RD.

A

B

C

WARWICK

A.V.

WARWICK

CHIPPENHAM

GOLDNEY

RD.

MARYLANDS RD.

6 414

FORMOSA

FORMOSA ST.

1

A404 18 36B

SUTHERLAND

ROAD

HARROW

182

Grand Union Canal Towpath

Canal

Walk

BLOMFIELD

DELAMERE

2

ALFRED RD.

RD.

SENIOR ST.

18 36

BOURNE

TER.

BLOM.

FIELD

HARROW

W

WESTWAY

3

A4207

WESTBOURNE PARK RD.

WESTBOURNE

WESTBOURNE PARK VILLAS

PARK ROAD

Royal Oak

SHREWSBURY RD.

CHEPSTOW

PARK

ROAD

ALEXANDER ST.

GLOUCESTER

RANE

LACH

TER.

PORCHESTER

CHESTER SQ.

POR.

TER. NTH.

ORS

4

TALBOT

7 28 31 70 328

HEREFORD

ROAD

SUNDERLAND TER.

WESTBOURNE GR.

Leisure Centre

Porchester Hall

PORCHESTER RD.

BISHOP'S

ARTESIAN

RD.

ROAD

70 W'bound

WESTBOURNE

GROVE

Dominican Republic

INVERNESS

5

23

WESTBOURNE GRO.

7 23 27

Space Apart

Whiteleys Centre

QUEENS

70

81

27 28

31 328

CHEPSTOW

PEMBRIDGE VILLAS

ROAD

LEINSTER SQ.

GARWAY RD.

Lords

Garden Court

GARDENS

KENSINGTON SQ.

Odeon

PORCHESTER G.

Whitelea

QUEENSBO

70

CHEPSTOW VS.

PEMBRIDGE PL.

A

31 328

76

New Linden

lace Court

PRINCES

Bayswater

B

SQ.

Phoenix

Kensington Gardens

C

Britannia Ct.

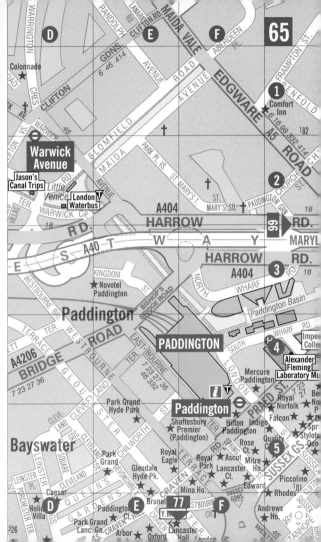

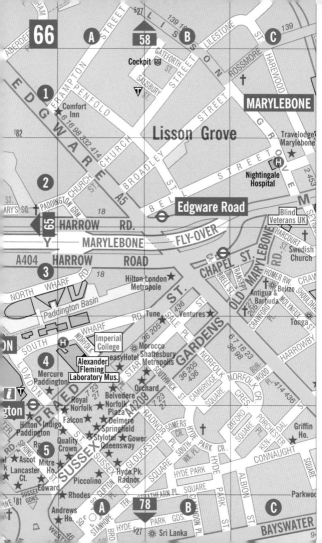

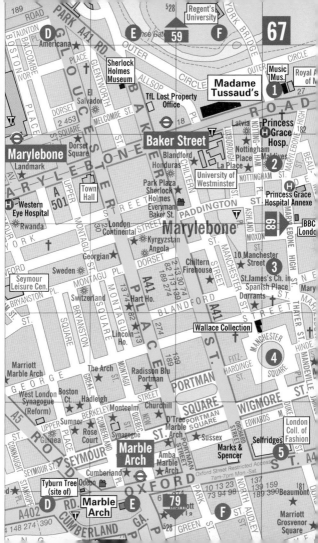

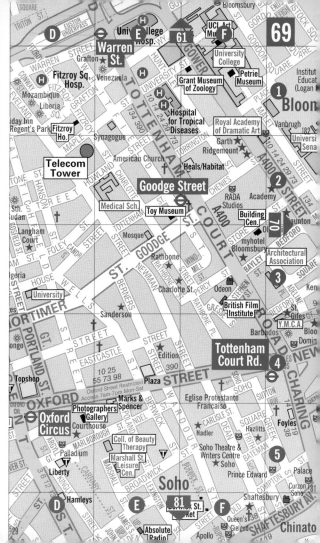

SQUARE
TRITON SQ

D EUSTON UNDERPASS

E University College Hosp.

UCL Art Museum F

GORDON ST ENDSLEIGH GDNS

ENDSLEIGH GDNS

TAVISTOCK

Bloomsbury

Warren St.

FITZROY WARREN STREET

Grafton

61

GOWER

University College

Petrie Museum

Institut Educat (Logan

1 Bloom

H Fitzroy Sq. Hosp.

CONWAY ST

FITZROY

EUSTON ST

CLEVELAND

Mozambique

Liberia

Venezuela

H

UNIVERSITY STREET

Grant Museum of Zoology

HUNTLEY

Royal Academy of Dramatic Art

Garth Ridgemount

10 14 24 29 73 Vanbrugh

Universi Sena

182

Hospital for Tropical Diseases

TOTTENHAM

10 14 24 73 390

liday Inn Regent's Park

Fitzroy Ho.

MAPLE

GRAFTON

Synagogue

American Church

Heals/Habitat

TORRINGTON

A400

Telecom Tower

HOWLAND

CHARLOTTE

COURT

Goodge Street

CHENIES

RADA Studios

Academy

2 STREET

STONE

HANSON ST

Sth. Judan

Langham Court

FOLEY

CANDR.

WELLS

TOTTENHAM

Medical Sch.

Toy Museum

GOODGE

Mosque

STREET

WIND-MILL

STORE

Building Cen.

myhotel Bloomsbury

70 BEDFORD

Staunton

rgeria

HOUSE

Rathbone

Charlotte St.

PERCY

BAYLEY

Architectural Association

3 SQUARE

ADELINE

BEDFORD

Ken

University

BERNERS

NEWMAN

RATHBONE PL

Odeon

GRESSE

STEPHEN

British Film Institute

St. Giles

Y.M.C.A.

Bloo

Domin

ongo

Sanderson

PORTLAND

GT.

STREET

EAST CASTLE

Edition

390

Tottenham Court Rd.

4 NEW

CHARING

Barbados

RTIMER

Topshop

OXFORD

10 25 55 73 98

Oxford Street Restricted Access 7am-7pm Mon-Sat

Plaza

STREET

SOHO

Eglise Protestante Française

74 38

OXFORD CIR.

Oxford Circus

Photographers' Gallery

Courthouse

Marks & Spencer

SOHO

BERWICK

NOEL

D'ARBLAY

DEAN

Nadler

CARLISLE ST.

Hazlitts

SQUARE

Foyles

19

Palladium

GT.

MARLBOROUGH

Coll. of Beauty Therapy

Marshall St. Leisure Cen.

BROADWICK

WARDOUR

BERWICK

Soho Theatre & Writers Centre

Soho

Prince Edward

FRITH

DEAN

GREEK

5

Liberty

CARNABY

D Hamleys

KINGLY

E

Soho

81 Berwick St. Market

F

Prince Edward

Curzon Soho

Palace

Shaftesbury

Queen's

Gielgud

SHAFTESBURY AV

Chinato

Absolute Radio

Apollo

599

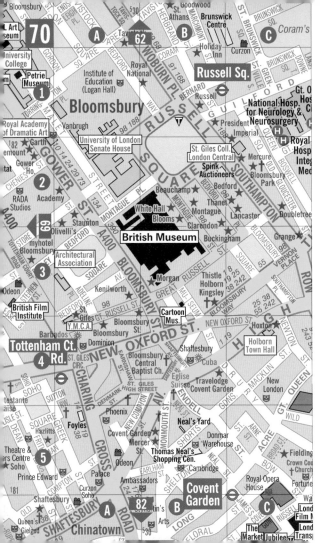

Mecklenburgh Sq. Gdns.
Fields

Club GRAY'S
CALTHORP
GOUGH
ENX
Mount Pleasant

Post Mus.
63
F

71

D
E

FARRINGDON
DOWLING

STREET
DOUGHTY
MILLMAN
Grenville

The Charles Dickens Mus.

Independent Television News

PLEASANT
WARNER
RAY ST.
HILL
BACK

ROSEBERY
1

rmond St. ospital for hildren

ROGER
JOHN ST.
Rugby St.
Kosovo
Malawi

INN

MOUNT
19 38 341
CLERKENWELL
ROAD
182

London ital for grated icine

DOMBEY ST.
NORTH
NEW
CONDUIT
GT. JAMES
BEDFORD
NORTHINGTON ST.

ROAD

55
London Weather Centre

LEATHER
HATTON

CROS
2
Fa

ST.
STREET
LANE

19 38
55 243

JOCKEY'S
Gray's Inn Gardens

Gray's Inn

ROAD

55
17 45
46 341

DORRING TON ST.

72

THEOBALD'S
RED LION
DRAKE
Conway Hall
Sierra Leone

PRINCETON
BEDFORD
Hall
Library

†

CROMPTON
GARDEN

CATTON
EAGLE
SQ.
PROCTER ST.

ROW
BROWNLOW ST.

Chancery Lane

BROOKE ST.

LEATHER LA.

98

8 25 242 521

HOLBORN
London Silver Vaults

HOLBORN
3 A40
HOLB
CI

Rosewood
Sir John Soane's Museum
Holborn

CHANCERY

STAPLE INN
STAPLE INN BS.

FURNIVAL
FETTER
NEW FETTER
A4

KINGS
REMNANT
Lincoln's Inn Library
Hall

Holborn
Lincoln's Inn Fields

CURSITOR
BREAM'S BLDGS.
4
341
Dr. John Hous

59 168 171
LINCOLN'S INN
SERLE

Kingsway Hall
Old Curiosity Shop
Royal College of Surgeons
CAREY

King's College Library

LA

Freemasons Hall
Peacock
Hunterian Museum
PORTUGAL

Royal Courts of Justice

FETTER
FLEET ST.
5
3 26
Apex

on Novello Mus. One Aldwych
Duchess

Theatre Royal Drury Lane
Aldwych

London School of Economics
Australia House

Temple Bar
FLEET ST.
341

Prince Henry's Room
Temple Hall
Inner Temple
Poland
182
Library

D
KEMBLE ST.
SARDINIA

ALDWYCH
India House
Bush House

E
83

STRAND

ARUNDEL

Hall Libr
Middle Temple
F

The Temple

Duchess
on port

Two Temple Place
Inner Temple

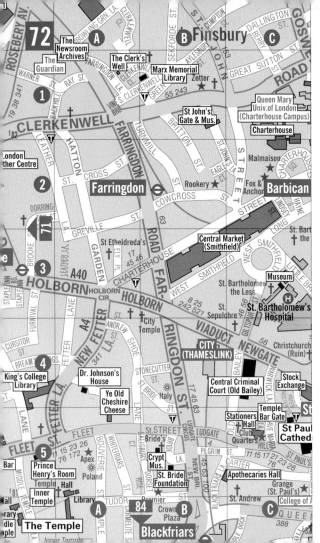

Finsbury

A **B** **C**

ROSEBERY AV.
GOSWELL ROAD
BOWLING GRN. LA.
CLERKENWELL CL.
CLERKENWELL RD.
ST. COMPTON ST.
DALLINGTON ST.
BERRY ST.

The Newsagent Archives
The Guardian
WARNER ST.
RAY ST.
BACKHILL
BRITTON ST.
The Clerk's Well
Marx Memorial Library
Zetter
SEKFORDE ST.
AYLESBURY
ST. JOHN
GREAT SUTTON ST.

1

CLERKENWELL
FARRINGDON
St John's Gate & Mus.
Queen Mary Univ. of London (Charterhouse Campus)
Charterhouse
CLERKENWELL GREEN
55 243
19 38 341
182
HATTON

LEATHER
CROSS ST.
TURNMILL ST.
Malmaison
CHARTERHOUSE SQ.
HAYNE
LINDSEY

2

London ther Centre
DORRING
LA.
GREVILLE
ST.
GARDEN
Rookery
COWCROSS
63
Fox & Anchor
Barbican
ST. JOHN ST.
EAGLE CT.
STREET
LONG LA.

Farringdon

3

BROOKE ST.
St Etheldreda's
17 45 46
ELY CT.
Central Market (Smithfield)
St. Bart the
LEATHER LA.
STAPLE INN BS.
STAPLE INN
A40
CHARTERHOUSE
WEST SMITHFIELD
Museum
LITTLE BR.
HOLBORN
HOLBORN CIR.
HOLBORN
FARRINGDON ROAD
8 25
242 521
St. Bartholomew the Less
St. Bartholomew's Hospital

4

CURSITOR ST.
FURNIVAL ST.
BREAM'S
NEW FETTER LANE
FETTER LA.
ANDREW ST.
SHOE LA.
341
City Temple
St. Sepulchre
46 56
VIADUCT
NEWGATE
56
Christchurch (Ruin)
King's College Library
Dr. Johnson's House
STONECUTTER ST.
CITY (THAMESLINK)
Central Criminal Court (Old Bailey)
OLD BAILEY
WARWICK LA.
AVE MARIA
Stock Exchange
Ye Old Cheshire Cheese
ST. BRIDE ST.
Italy
17 45 63
Stationers' Hall
Temple Bar Gate
St Paul's Cathedral
St

5

Bar
Prince Henry's Room
Temple Hall
Inner Temple Library
FLEET LANE
MIDDLE TEMPLE
BOUVERIE ST.
WHITEFRIARS
SALISBURY CT.
FLEET ST.
STREET
St. Bride's
Crypt Mus.
BRIDE LA.
St. Bride Foundation
LUDGATE CIRCUS
LUDGATE HILL
PILGRIM ST.
NEW BRIDGE ST.
DORSET RISE
4
CARTER LA.
11 15 17 21 23 26
ST. PAUL'S
Club Quarters
Apothecaries Hall
Grange (St. Paul's)
College of A
St. Andrew
11 15 23 26 76 172
Apex Poland
TUDOR ST.
Premier
BLACK FRIARS LA.

A **B** **C**

The Temple
84
Blackfriars
Crown Plaza
QUEEN
Inner Temple

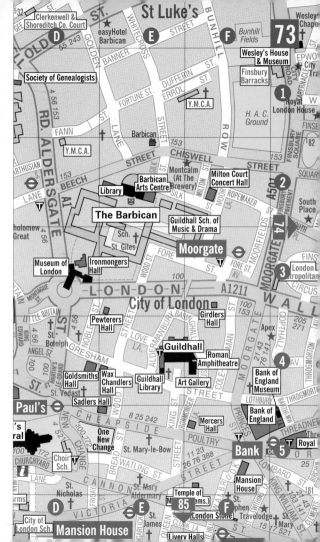

74

CITY RD.

Wesleys Chapel

A **B** **C**

Wesley's House & Museum

Finsbury Barracks **1**

Royal London House

H. A. C. Ground

Shoredith

LUKE STREET

EPWORTH ST.

SCRUTTON ST.

GREAT EASTERN STREET

HOLYWELL LA.

City Road Travelodge

FOLGATE

Dennis

Ho

WORSHIP

FINSBURY SQUARE

CHRISTOPHER ST.

FINSBURY PAVEMENT

CLIFTON ST.

APPOLD

SHOREDITCH HIGH

Tune

PRIMROSE ST.

SPITAL SQ.

Charnel House

STREET **2**

n Court cert Hall

A501

SUN ST.

BROADGATE

Broadgate Circle

BRUSHFIE

Bishops Inst. &

Synagogue

SOUTH PL.

St. Mary

ELDON ST.

LIVERPOOL STREET

Rav

G

Dirty Dicks

FINSBURY CIRCUS

London Metropolitan Uni. **3**

BLOMFIELD

LIVERPOOL

AND4Z

MIDDLESEX

Liverpool St.

St. Botolph

Travelodge

LONDON A1211 WALL

COPTHALL AV.

Apex

WORMWOOD STREET

Heron Tower

HOUNDSDITC

eatre

THROGMORTON

Carpenters Hall

Dutch Church

Tower 42

BROAD

St Ethelburga

Pet Sunda

Bank of England Museum **4**

Drapers Hall

St Helens

Bevis Marks Synagogue

THROGMORTON ST.

OLD

"The Cheesegrater"

"The Gherkin"

St. Andrew

LOTHBURY

Bank of England

THREADNEEDLE

Merchant Taylors Hall

Lloyds Registry

Threadneedles

Bank 5

Royal Exchange

CORNHILL

St. Michael Club Quarters

Lloyds Building

Lloyds Registry

Mansion House

LOMBARD

Leadenhall Market

FENCHURCH

St Stephen one

Travelodge

St. Mary

A **86** **B** **C** **FENCHUR**

Cloth Workers Hall

"The Walkie-Talkie"

St. Margaret

Synagogue

GREEN ST.   DUNBRIDGE ST.

BETHNAL GREEN ROAD   B 388

D   SCLATER ST.   **E**   CHESHIRE   **F**

(!) Shoreditch High St.

Brick Lane Sunday Market (am)

WHEELER   QUAKER   ST.   BUXTON   STREET   **1**

LAMB   ST.   SPITAL   ST.   DEAL   †   182

Old Truman Brewery

Severs' House

HANBURY   **Spitalfields**   STREET   **2**

Old Spitalfields Market   Mosque ☐   GREATOREX

FOURNIER   ST.   DAVENANT   STREET

sgate Liby.   Old London Fruit Exchange   † Christ Church Spitalfields   East London Mosque

n Row allery   FASHION   ST.   CHICKSAND   MONTAGUE   ST.   **3** Syn.

BELL LA.   OLD   WHITECHAPEL RD.   FIELDGATE ST.   GREENFIELD RD.

A1202   STREET   67   STREET   OSBORN ST.   A11   WHITECHAPEL   25 106   ADLER ST.

ipettcoat Lane   WENTWORTH   Toynbee Hall   London Metropolitan University   **4**

ticoat Lane y Market (am)   OLD CASTLE   Ibis ★   Whitechapel Art Gallery   WHITE CH. LA.

Aldgate East   WHITECHAPEL HIGH ST.   MANNINGTREE LA.   COMMERCIAL   ROAD

15 25 100   BRAH-AM ST.   GOODMANS STILE   A13   15 15B 40

ST BOTOLPH STREET   135 205   LEMAN   GOWER'S   BACK CHURCH LANE

Aldgate   ALDGATE HIGH ST.   15 42 78 100   †   **Whitechapel**

RCH ST   Bus Station   MANSELL   ALIE   GOODMANS   WALK   **5**

JEWRY   London Metropolitan University   A1210   LEMAN STREET   15 42 78 100   FAIRCLOUGH ST.

Indigo,   Chamberlain   A1202   HOOPER   ELLEN ST.   181

FRIARS INDIA ST.   PORTSOKEN ST.   **E** ★ Premier   **87**   **F**   Mosque

CH ST   CROSSWA...   RV1   Inn   STREET   534   LANE   CABLE STREET

GOODMANS YARD   CHAMBER...

Travelodge

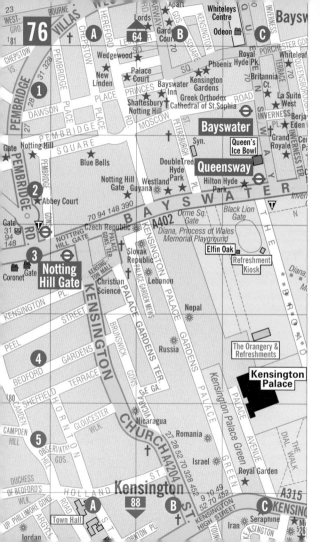

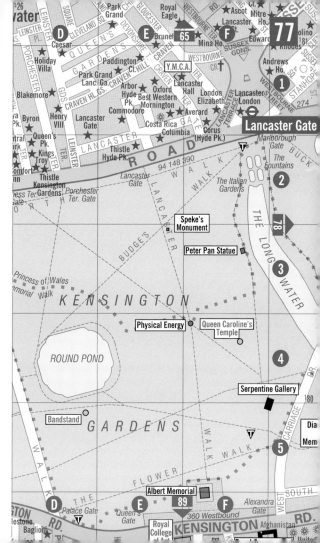

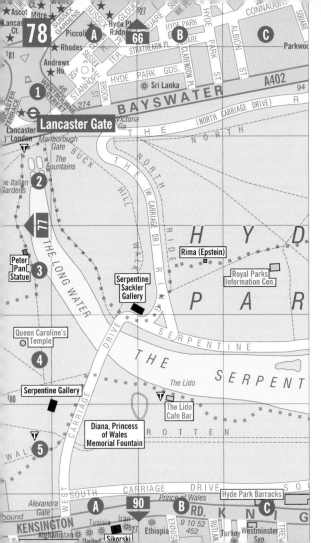

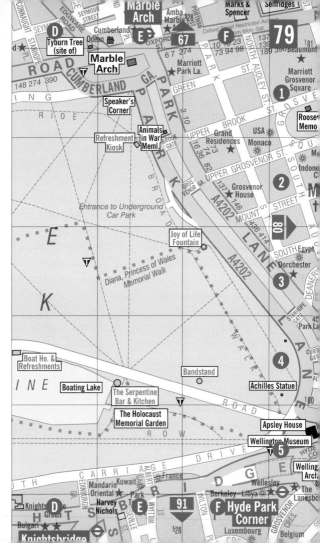

Marble
Arch

Amba
Marble ★ 528

Marks &
Spencer

Selfridges

D Tyburn Tree
(site of)

Cumberland
Odeon

E OXFORD
ST.

67

Oxford Street Restricted Access
from Mon.-Sat.

F

137
139
189 390 Beaumont

67 274

73 94 98 NORTH

10 18 23

Marble
Arch

CONNAUGHT

SEYMOUR STREET

EDGWARE ROAD

STANHOPE PL.

ROAD

148 274 390

CUMBERLAND

GA.

PARK

GREEN

Marriott
Park La. ★

ST.

AUDLEY

SOUTH

NORTH

Marriott
Grosvenor
Square

1

GROSVE

Roose
Memo

Speaker's
Corner ★

2.10

Animals
in War
Meml.

Refreshment
Kiosk ◇

RIDE

PARK

BROOK
GATE

UPPER

BROOK

Grand
Residences

16 36 82

USA ☀

Grand

GROSVENOR ST.

Monaco

SOUTH

SQU

Indone
C

BROAD

GROS-
VENOR GA.

UPPER GROSVENOR ST.

137 ★

Grosvenor
House

148 ★

MOUNT

STREET

2

M

Entrance to Underground
Car Park

A4202

80

Joy of Life
Fountain ○

A4202

SOUTH

Egypt

3

Dorchester ★

DEANER

Diana, Princess of Wales
Memorial Walk

▽

E

K

STANHOPE
GATE

45
Park La

WALK

Boat Ho. &
Refreshments

INE

Boating Lake

Bandstand
○

LANE

CUR
GA

4

Achilles Statue ★

The Serpentine
Bar & Kitchen

▽

ROAD

180

The Holocaust
Memorial Garden

ROW

Apsley House ■

Wellington Museum ■

5

HYDE
CO

CARRIAGE

DRIVE

G

Welling
Arch

S
O
U
T
H

EDINBURGH
GA.

ALBERT

Mandarin
Oriental

Kuwait

France ☀

WILTON

Park

Berkeley

Libya ☀

Wellesley

The
Lanesb

BRIDGE

GROSVENOR
CRES.

Knights
Green

D

Harvey
Nichols

E

WILLIAM
ST.

SEVILE

91

528

F Hyde Park
Corner

Luxembourg

Belgium

HO T

Bulgari ★★

Knightsbridge

▽ 528

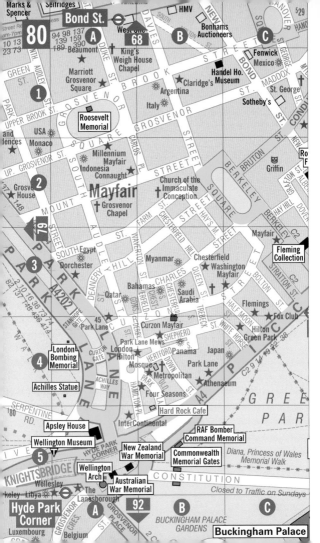

Marks & Spencer
Selfridges

80

94 98 137
139 159
189 390

10 13
23 73

Bond St.

West one

HMV

Bonhams
Auctioneers

NEW

HANOVER

A

68

B

C

529

Fenwick
Mexico

Beaumont

King's
Weigh House
Chapel

Marriott
Grosvenor Square

Claridge's

Handel Ho.
Museum

St. George

DUKE

ST.

BROOK

STREET

BOND

MADDOX

ST.

Sotheby's

CONDI

Roosevelt
Memorial

Argentina

Italy

GROSVENOR

STREET

BERKELEY

BRUTON

Griffin

GREEN

ST.

1

USA

Monaco

Millennium
Mayfair
Indonesia
Connaught

SQUARE

STREET

SQUARE

HAY HILL

BERKELEY

DOVER

Mayfair

C2

Fleming
Collection

C2

fences

UPPER BROOK ST.

UP. GROSVENOR ST.

AUDLEY

GROSVENOR

2

Grosvenor
House

148

Mayfair

Grosvenor
Chapel

Church of the
Immaculate
Conception

FARM

ST.

CHESTERFIELD HILL

HAY'S M.

STREET

MOUNT

STREET

SOUTH

SOUTH

79

Egypt
Dorchester

Myanmar

Chesterfield

Washington
Mayfair

BOLTON

STREET

STRATTON ST.

Flemings

Fox Club

C2

3

2 10 16 36
137 148 436 419

Qatar

WAVERTON ST.

DEANERY ST.

Bahamas

CHARLES

CHESTERFIELD

Saudi
Arabia

QUEEN

HALF MOON

WHITE HORSE

ST.

Hilton
Green Park

C

38

A4202

PARK

LANE

SOUTH

Dorchester

CURZON

ST.

HERTFORD

CHESTFIELD

FRIEDLAND

Curzon Mayfair

Panama

Park Lane
Mews

London
Hilton

SHEPHERD

Japan

Park Lane

C

29 14 9 22 38

STANHOPE GATE

45
Park Lane

CURZON GATE

London
Mosque

Metropolitan

4

London
Bombing
Memorial

Achilles Statue

HAMILTON

STREET

ACHILLES
WAY

PL.

Four Seasons

Athenaeum

A4

P

C

GREE

PAR

SERPENTINE
RD.

180

Apsley House

Wellington Museum

5

HYDE PARK
CORNER

New Zealand
War Memorial

Hard Rock Cafe

InterContinental

RAF Bomber
Command Memorial

Commonwealth
Memorial Gates

Diana, Princess of Wales
Memorial Walk

KNIGHTSBRIDGE

Wellesley

keley · Libya

The
Lanesborough

Wellington
Arch

Australian
War Memorial

CONSTITUTION

Closed to Traffic on Sundays

**Hyde Park
Corner**

Luxembourg

GROSVENOR CRES.

GROSVENOR
PLACE

ST.

A

92

B

BUCKINGHAM PALACE
GARDENS

C

Buckingham Palace

Belgium

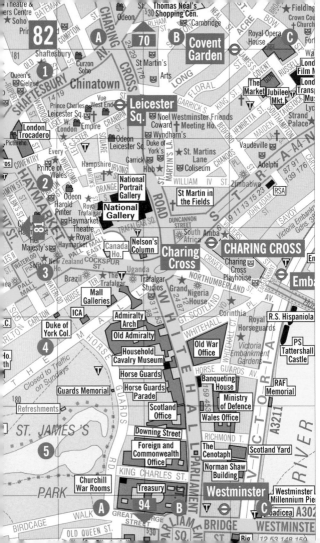

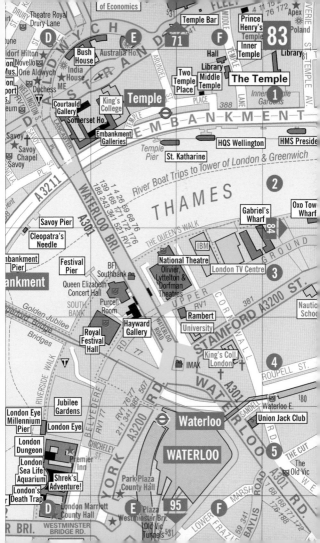

of Economics

Theatre Royal
Drury Lane
D

Bush
House

Australia Ho.

India
House

King's
College

Temple Bar

71

Prince
Henry's
Temple
Inner
Temple
F

83

4 11 15
76 172

Apex
Poland

Hall

Library

The Temple

Inner
Temple
Gardens

Library

E

One Aldwych

Duchess

Temple

Courtauld
Gallery

Somerset Ho.

Embankment
Galleries

Two
Temple
Place

Middle
Temple

1

388

E M B A N K M E N T

Temple
Pier

St. Katharine

HQS Wellington

HMS Preside

River Boat Trips to Tower of London & Greenwich

2

Savoy Pier

Cleopatra's
Needle

THE QUEEN'S WALK

T H A M E S

Gabriel's
Wharf

Oxo Tow
Wharf

84

Festival
Pier

BFI
Southbank

IBM

National Theatre
Olivier,
Lyttelton &
Dorfman
Theatres

London TV Centre

3

Embankment
Pier

ankment

Golden Jubilee
Bridges

Queen Elizabeth
Concert Hall

Purcell
Room

Hayward
Gallery

SOUTH
BANK

UPPER
GROUND

Rambert
University

RV1

CORNWALL

381

Nautic
Scho

4

Royal
Festival
Hall

RIVERSIDE WALK

IMAX

King's Coll.
London

STAMFORD A3200 ST.

WATERLOO

ROUPELL ST.

London Eye
Millennium
Pier

Jubilee
Gardens

London Eye

Waterloo E.

Waterloo

Union Jack Club

180

SANDELL

5

London
Dungeon

London
Sea Life
Aquarium

London's
Death Trap

D

Shrek's
Adventure!

Premier
Inn

Park Plaza
County Hall

CHICHELEY

WATERLOO

THE CUT

The
Old Vic

WE

London Marriott
County Hall

WESTMINSTER
BRIDGE RD.

BRI.

E

YORK

A3200

Plaza
Westminster Bri.
Old Vic
Tunnels

95

F

MARSH

LOWER FRAZI

BAYLIS

1 68 168 171 12
176 12

A301

RD.

Prince

Room Hall

Temple

Library

Apex
Polan

11 15 17 21 23 26
ST. PAUL'S

CARTER

Crypt Mus.

St. Bride Foundation

72

Apothecaries Hall

range
(St. Paul's)

St. Andrew

C

The Temple

1 Inner Temple Gardens

Premier Inn

Crowne Plaza

Blackfriars

QUEEN
388

TUDOR

TEMPLE AV.

CARMELITE ST.

BLACKFRIARS UNDERPASS

UPPER

WHITE LION HILL

RIVERSIDE

VICTORIA EMBANKMENT

388

HQS Wellington

HMS President

Blackfriars Pier

BLACKFRIARS

River Boat Trips to Tower of London & Greenwich

2 R I V E R

45 63 100

BLACKFRIARS BRI.

A201 BLACKFRIARS

T H

Gabriel's f

83

Oxo Tower Wharf

Mondrian

GROUND
RV1

Bankside Gallery

THE QUEEN'S

Tate Modern

London TV Centre

3

UPPER

HOPTON

HOLLAND

SUMNER

ST.

SOUTHWARK

CORNWALL

STAMFORD
A3200

381

Nautical School

The Mad Hatter

Sports Centre

BURREL ST.

BEAR

RV1 381

Holiday Inn Express

Hilton

Me
Lo

Applied Arts

LAVINGTON

Premier Inn

ing's Coll London

4

ROUPELL ST.

MEYMOTT ST.

ST. Ibis & Novotel

Southwark

Southwark

BRAD

WATERLOO EAST

CUT

UNION

A201 ROAD

Union

Southwark Travelodge

Jerwood Space Galle

180

Waterloo E.

Union Jack Club

Young Vic

Lewisham College

COPPERFIE

Blackfriars

WATERLOO

THE

CUFFORD

SURREY ROW

POCOCK

STREE

SUFFOLK

00

5

MARSHAM ROAD

A301

BAYLIS

FRAZII

59 341

WEBBER ROW

The Old Vic

Hampton by Hilton

96

Travelodge

Teacher

EBBER RW.

LANCAS

STREE

532

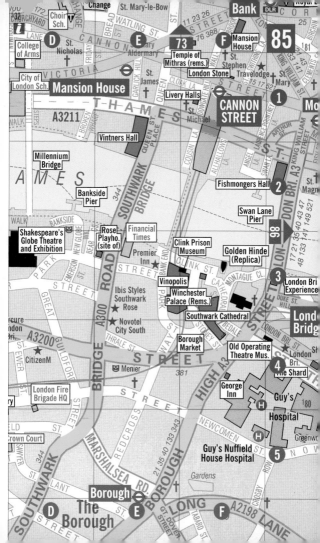

ORCHARD
Choir Sch.
172
Change
St. Mary-le-Bow
WATLING ST.
11 23 26
76 388
Bank
DLR
COR
CANNON
BREAD
ST.
STREET
25
LANE
FRIDAY
CANNON
St.
Mary
Aldermary
St.
James
73
F
Mansion
House
85
D
St.
Nicholas
E
Temple of
Mithras (rems.)
St.
Stephen
London Stone
Travelodge
181
College
of Arms
GARLICK HILL
VICTORIA
St.
Michael
St. Mary
City of
London Sch.
Mansion House
CLOAK LA.
Livery Halls
DOWGATE HILL
CANNON
STREET
1
THAMES
A3211
QUEEN PLACE
STEPS
WALK
BROKEN
Vintners Hall
ARTHUR
ST.
KING WILLIAM ST.
Mo
A ME S
Millennium
Bridge
Bankside
Pier
COUSIN LA.
ALLHALLOWS
Fishmongers Hall
LON
BRI.
A3
St.
Magn
2
SWAN LA.
ANGEL
Swan Lane
Pier
BANKSIDE
WALK
344
SOUTHWARK
BRIDGE
17 21 35 40 43 47
48 133 141 149 521
Shakespeare's
Globe Theatre
and Exhibition
NEW GLOBE
BEAR GD.
Rose
Playho.
(site of)
Financial
Times
Clink Prison
Museum
Golden Hinde
(Replica)
98
LONDON
STREET
A3
3
London Bri
Experience
PARK
EMERSON
STREET
Premier
Inn
PARK ST.
BANK END
Vinopolis
CLINK ST.
MONTAGUE CL.
DUKE ST.
HILL
Lond
Bridg
WINCHESTER
Ibis Styles
Southwark
Rose
Novotel
City South
Winchester
Palace (Rems.)
Southwark Cathedral
LONDON BRI ST.
London Bri.
ercure
ndon
ri.
A3200
GUILDFOR
CitizenM
THRALE ST.
BRIDGE
A300
PARK
STREET
STONEY ST.
REDEDALE
BEDALE
Borough
Market
STREET
Old Operating
Theatre Mus.
4
The Shard
London
St
HIGH A3
London Fire
Brigade HQ
Menier
BOROUGH
381
George
Inn
H
Guy's
180
Hospital
Greenwe
ry
Crown Court
SAWYER
ST.
A3200
MARSHALSEA RD.
REDCROSS
WAY
BOROUGH
NEWCOMEN
Guy's Nuffield
House Hospital
Gardens
ST.
NOV
5
H
21 35 40 133 343
344
LANT
ST.
CROSBY ROW
SOUTHWARK
D
The
Borough
E
Borough
GT. DOVER
STREET
LONG
F
A2198 LANE
TABARD

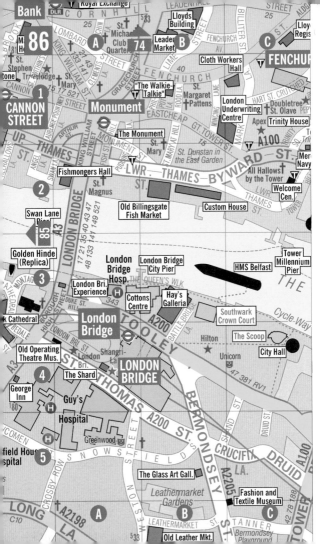

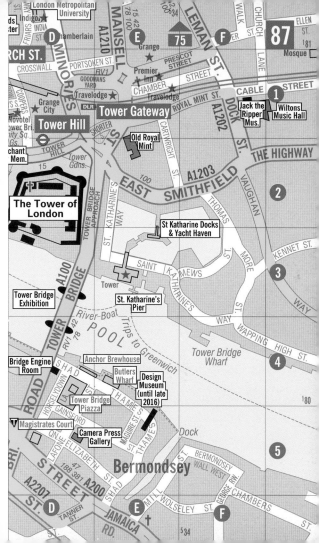

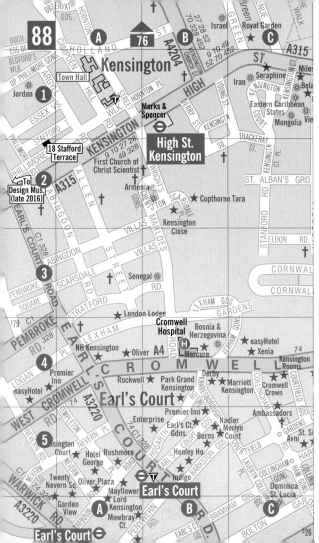

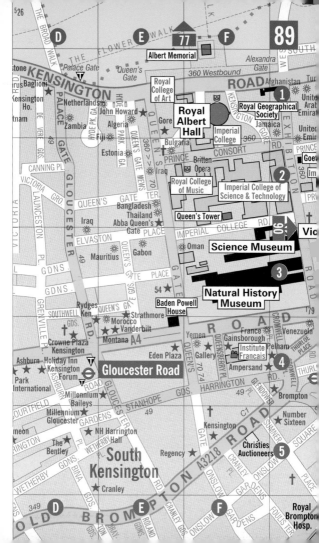

THE BROAD WALK

FLOWER WALK

Albert Memorial

Alexandra Gate

Palace Gate

Queen's Gate

360 Westbound

ROAD

Afghanistan

Tur

KENSINGTON

Baglioni

stone

Kensington Ho.

Netherlands

Royal College of Art

HYDE PK GA

John Howard ★

Algeria

Unite
Arab
Emira

1

Royal Geographical Society

Jamaica

Royal Albert Hall

PALACE

tnam

DE VERE GDS.

Zambia

Gore

Fiji ★

QUEEN'S GATE

Imperial College 360

United
Emir

GOR

Goet

Estonia ★

Bulgaria

CONSORT

PRINCE

Im

CANNING PL.

GATE

Iraq

Britten
Opera

PRI

GLOUCESTER

360 V V

Royal College of Music

2

Imperial College of Science & Technology

360

VICTORIA

GRO

QUEEN'S

GATE TER.

Bangladesh

70

Queen's Tower

LAUNCESTON

49

Thailand
Abba Queen's ★

PL.

Iraq

ELVASTON

Gate PLACE

IMPERIAL

COLLEGE

RD.

90

Vic

PLACE

Mauritius

Gabon

Oman

Science Museum

3

QUEEN'S

GDNS.

GATE

PLACE

GDNS.

54 ★

SGB

Baden Powell House

Natural History Museum

RO AD

179

GRENVILLE PL.

Rydges

QUEEN'S GATE

SOUTHWELL Ken

Morocco

Strathmore

CROMWELL

France ★

Venezuela

Yemen

Vanderbilt

Gainsborough

Pelhan

THURLO
PLACE

Crowne Plaza
Kensington

Montana A4

Queensborough

Institute
Francais

THURL

Ashburn Holiday Inn
Kensington Forum

Eden Plaza

Gallery

Ampersand

RD.

4

Brompton

Park
International

Millennium

ASHBURN

ROAD

HARRINGTON

PL.

49

Number
Sixteen

Baileys

STANHOPE

GDS.

GDNS

SQUAR

COURTFIELD

Millennium
Gloucester

GARDENS

49

meon

NH Harrington
Hall

WETHERBY

PL.

Kensington

C.1

Christies
Auctioneers

5

RINGTON

The ★
Bentley

Regency ★

GATE

A3218

ROAD

SINNER

PLACE

South Kensington

BINA

Cranley ★

ONSLOW

ROLAND

GDNS

ONSLOW GARDENS

FOULIS

WETHERBY

GDNS.

349

D

BROMPTON

F

Royal
Brompton
Hosp.

OLD

CRANLEY

Gloucester Road

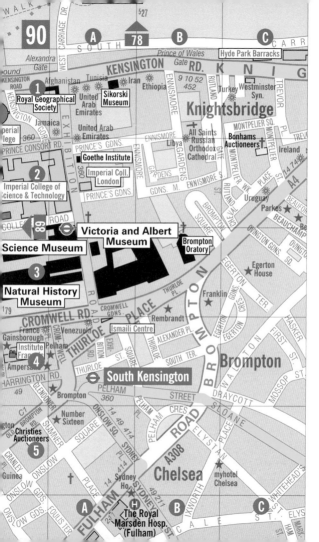

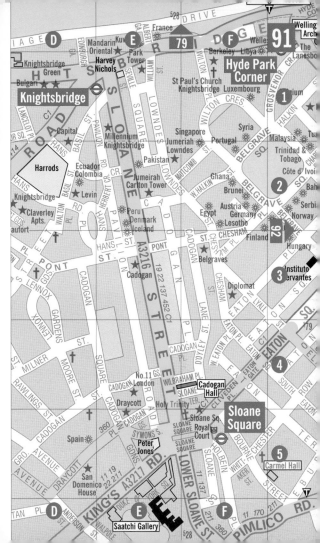

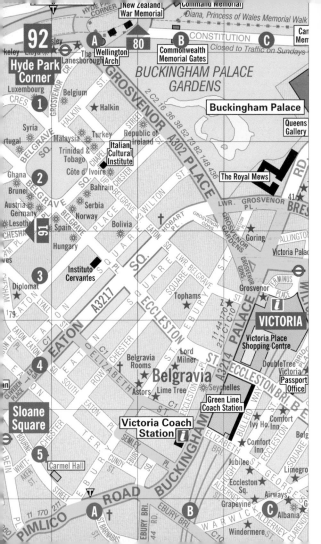

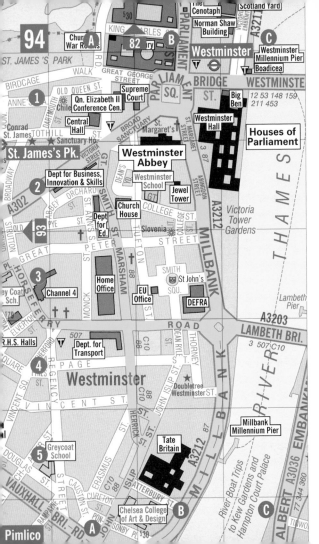

ST. JAMES'S PARK

KING CHARLES ST

The Cenotaph
Scotland Yard
Norman Shaw Building

Westminster

Westminster Millennium Pier
Boadicea

A Chur War Rms

82 try **B**

C VICTORIA EMBANKMENT A3211

BIRDCAGE WALK

GREAT GEORGE STREET

BRIDGE ST.

BRIDGE **WESTMINSTE**

PARLIAMENT SQ.

ANNE'S

OLD QUEEN ST

1

TE Chile

Conrad St. James

DARTMOUTH

TOTHILL

Qn. Elizabeth II Conference Cen.

Central Hall

Supreme Court

St. Margaret's

Big Ben

Westminster Hall

12 53 148 159 211 453

Houses of Parliament

Sanctuary Ho

BROAD SANCTUARY

MARGARET STREET

BROADWAY

St. James's Pk.

VICTORIA STREET

Westminster Abbey

ABINGDON STREET

2 Dept for Business, Innovation & Skills

Westminster School

A3212

A302

ABBEY

ORCHARD ST.

SMITH ST.

ST. ANN'S ST.

Jewel Tower

Victoria Tower Gardens

93 PYE

Dept for Ed.

Church House

COLLEGE

GT. ST.

T H A M E S

GREAT

PETER

TUFTON

Slovenia

STREET

MILLBANK

HORSEFERRY

MARSHAM

Lambeth Pier

3

ey Coat Sch.

Channel 4

Home Office

St John's SQU.

EU Office

DEFRA

A3203

ELVERTON ST.

MONCK

ROAD

LAMBETH BRI.

R.H.S. Halls

507

Dept. for Transport

DEAN RYLE ST.

THORNEY

3 507 C10

4 Westminster

PAGE

REGENCY ST.

C10 88

DOUBLETREE Westminster ST.

RIVER

VINCENT SQ.

VINCENT ST.

88 C10

Doubletree Westminster

JOHN ISLIP ST.

HERRICK ST.

Tate Britain

Millbank Millennium Pier

A3212 87

5 Greycoat School

DOUGLAS ST.

ERASMUS ST.

River Boat Trips to Kew Gardens and Hampton Court Palace

A3036

ALBERT EMBANKMENT

VAUXHALL BRI. RD.

RAMPAYNE ST.

CAUSTON ST.

CURETON ST.

ATTERBURY

ST.

SONBY ST.

PONSONBY

A Chelsea College of Art & Design **B**

C

Pimlico

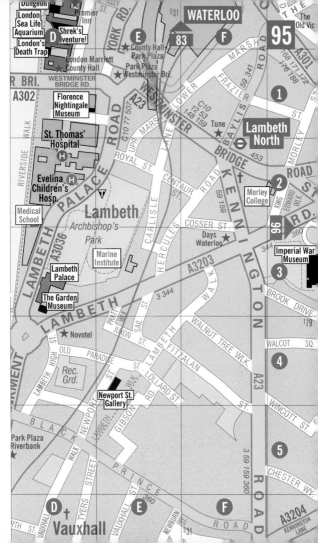

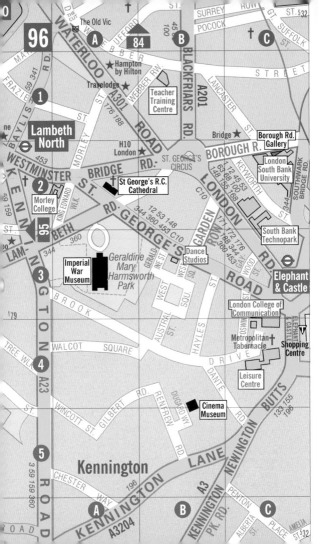

Abbreviations:

All : Alley
App : Approach
Arc : Arcade
Av : Avenue
Bk : Back
Boulevd : Boulevard
Bri : Bridge
B'way : Broadway
Bldgs : Buildings
Bus : Business
Cen : Centre
Chu : Church
Chyd : Churchyard
Circ : Circle
Cir : Circus
Clo : Close
Comn : Common
Cotts : Cottages

Ct : Court
Cres : Crescent
Dri : Drive
E : East
Embkmt : Embankment
Est.: Estate
Gdns : Gardens
Ga : Gate
Gt : Great
Grn : Green
Gro : Grove
Ho : House
Ind : Industrial
Junct : Junction
La : Lane
Lit : Little
Lwr : Lower
Mnr : Manor
Mans : Mansions
Mkt : Market

M : Mews
Mt : Mount
N : North
Pal : Palace
Pde : Parade
Pk : Park
Pas : Passage
Pl : Place
Rd : Road
S : South
Sq : Square
Sta : Station
St : Street
Ter : Terrace
Up : Upper
Vs : Villas
Wlk : Walk
W : West
Yd : Yard

Burlington Gdns. W1 —2D 81
Burrell St. SE1 —3B 84
Burwood Pl. W2 —4C 66
Buxton St. E1 —1E 75
Byward St. EC3 —2C 86

Cabbell St. NW1 —3B 66
Cable St. E1 —1F 87
Cadogan Gdns. SW3 —5E 91
Cadogan La. SW1 —3F 91
Cadogan Pl. SW1 —2E 91
Cadogan Sq. SW1 —3E 91
Cadogan St. SW3 —5D 91
Caledonian Rd. N1 —2C 62
Caledonia St. N1 —2C 62
Cale St. SW3 —5B 90
Calshot St. N1 —1D 63
Calthorpe St. WC1 —5E 63
Cambridge Sq. W2 —4B 66
Camden High St. NW1 —1D 61
Camden St. NW1 —1E 61
Camley St. N1 —1A 62
Camomile St. EC3 —2C 74
Campden Hill. W8 —5A 76
Candover St. W1 —3D 69
Canning Pl. W8 —2D 89
Cannon St. EC4 —5D 73
Carburton St. W1 —2C 68
Cardington St. NW1 —3E 61
Carey St. WC2 —5E 71
Carlisle La. SE1 —3E 95
Carlisle Pl. SW1 —3D 93
Carlisle St. W1 —5F 69
Carlos Pl. W1 —2A 80
Carlton Gdns. SW1 —4F 81
Carlton Ho. Ter. SW1 —3F 81
Carmelite St. EC4 —1A 84
Carnaby St. W1 —5D 69
Carnegie St. N1 —1E 63
Carter La. EC4 —5C 72
Carthusian St. EC1 —2D 73
Carting La. WC2 —2C 82
Cartwright Gdns. WC1 —4B 62
Cartwright St. E1 —2E 87
Castellain Rd. W9 —1C 64
Castle La. SW1 —2D 93
Cathedral Plazza. SW1 —3E 93
Cathedral St. SE1 —3F 85
Catton St. WC1 —3D 71
Causton St. SW1 —5A 94
Cavendish Av. NW8 —2A 58
Cavendish Clo. NW8 —3A 58
Cavendish Pl. W1 —4C 68
Cavendish Sq. W1 —4C 68
Caxton St. SW1 —2F 93
Centaur St. SE1 —2E 95
Chadwell St. EC1 —3F 63
Chalton St. NW1 —1E 61

Chamber St. E1 —1E 87
Chambers St. SE16 —5F 87
Chancery La. WC2 —4F 71
Chandos Pl. WC2 —2B 82
Chandos St. W1 —3C 68
Chapel Mkt. N1 —1F 63
Chapel St. NW1 —3B 66
Chapel St. SW1 —2A 92
Chapter St. SW1 —5F 93
Charing Cross Rd. WC2 —5A 70
Charlbert St. NW8 —1B 58
Charles II St. SW1 —3F 81
Charles St. W1 —3B 80
Charlotte St. W1 —2E 69
Charlotte Ter. N1 —1E 63
Charlwood St. SW1 —5E 93
(in two parts)
Charrington St. NW1 —2F 61
Charterhouse Sq. EC1 —2C 72
Charterhouse St. EC1 —3A 72
Cheapside. EC2 —5D 73
Chenies Pl. NW1 —1A 62
Chenies St. WC1 —2F 69
Cheniston Gdns. W8 —2B 88
Chepstow Pl. W2 —5A 64
Chepstow Rd. W2 —4A 64
Chepstow Vs. W11 —1A 76
Chesham Pl. SW1 —3F 91
Chesham St. SW1 —3F 91
Cheshire St. E2 —1E 75
Chesterfield Gdns. W1 —3B 80
Chesterfield Hill. W1 —2B 80
Chesterfield St. W1 —3B 80
Chester Ga. NW1 —4B 60
Chester Rd. NW1 —4A 60
Chester Row. SW1 —5A 92
Chester Sq. SW1 —4A 92
Chester St. SW1 —2A 92
Chester Ter. NW1 —3B 60
Chester Way. SE11 —5A 96
Chichley St. SW7 —2C 90
Chicheley St. SE1 —5E 83
Chicksand St. E1 —3E 75
(in two parts)
Chiltern St. W1 —2F 67
Chilton St. E2 —1E 75
Chilworth St. W2 —5E 65
Chippenham Rd. W9 —1A 64
Chiswell St. EC1 —2F 73
Christopher St. EC2 —1A 74
Church St. W2 —2A 66
Church St. NW8 —2A 66
Churchway. NW1 —3F 61
Churton St. SW1 —5E 93
Circus Rd. NW8 —3A 58
City Rd. EC1 —1A 74
Claremont Sq. N1 —2F 63
Clarendon Pl. W2 —1B 78
Clarendon St. SW1 —5C 92

Flower Wlk., The. SW7 —1E 89
Foley St. W1 —3D 69
Folgate St. E1 —2C 74
Fore St. EC2 —3E 73
Fore St. Av. EC2 —3F 73
Formosa St. W9 —1C 64
Fortune St. EC1 —1E 73
Foulis Ter. SW7 —5A 90
Fournier St. E1 —2E 75
Frampton St. NW8 —1A 66
Francis St. SW1 —4E 93
Frazier St. SE1 —1F 95
Frederick St. WC1 —4D 63
Friday St. EC4 —1D 85
Frith St. W1 —5F 69
Furnival St. EC4 —4F 71
Fynes St. SW1 —4F 93

Gainsford St. SE1 —5D 87
Garden Row. SE1 —2B 96
Garlick Hill. EC4 —1E 85
Garrick St. WC2 —1B 82
Garway Rd. W2 —5B 64
Gateforth St. NW8 —1A 66
Gaywood St. SE1 —3C 96
Gee St. EC1 —1D 73
George Row. SE16 —5F 87
George St. W1 —4D 67
Geraldine St. SE11 —3B 96
Gibson Rd. SE11 —5E 95
Gilbert Rd. SE11 —5A 96
Gillingham St. SW1 —4D 93
Giltspur St. EC1 —4C 72
Glasshouse St. W1 —2E 81
Glendower Pl. SW7 —4A 90
Glentworth St. NW1 —1D 67
Gloucester Ga. NW1 —1B 60
Gloucester Pl. NW1 & W1 —1D 67
Gloucester Rd. SW7 —2D 89
Gloucester Sq. W2 —5A 66
Gloucester St. SW1 —5D 93
Gloucester Ter. W2 —4C 64
Gloucester Wlk. W8 —5A 76
Godliman Street. EC4 —5D 73
Golden La. EC1 —1D 73
Golden Sq. W1 —1E 81
Goldington Cres. NW1 —1F 61
Goldington St. NW1 —1F 61
Goldney Rd. W9 —1A 64
Goodge St. W1 —3E 69
Goodmans Stile. E1 —4F 75
Goodmans Yd. E1 —1E 87
Goods Way. N1 —1B 62
Gordon Sq. WC1 —5F 61
Gordon St. WC1 —5F 61
Gosfield St. W1 —3D 69
Goswell Rd. EC1 —1C 72
Gough St. WC1 —5E 63

Gower Pl. WC1 —5E 61
Gower St. WC1 —5E 61
Gower's Wlk. E1 —4F 75
Gracechurch St. EC3 —1A 86
Grafton Pl. NW1 —4F 61
Grafton St. W1 —2C 80
Grafton Way. W1 & WC1 —1D 69
Granby Ter. NW1 —2D 61
Gray's Inn Rd. WC1 —3C 62
Gt. College St. SW1 —2B 94
Gt. Cumberland Pl. W1 —4D 67
Gt. Dover St. SE1 —5E 85
Gt. Eastern St. EC2 —1C 74
Gt. George St. SW1 —1A 94
Gt. Guildford St. SE1 —3D 85
Gt. James St. WC1 —2E 71
Gt. Marlborough St. W1 —5D 69
Greatorex St. E1 —2F 75
Gt. Ormond St. WC1 —2C 70
Gt. Percy St. WC1 —3E 63
Gt. Peter St. SW1 —3A 94
Gt. Portland St. W1 —1C 68
Gt. Queen St. WC2 —5C 70
Gt. Russell St. WC1 —4A 70
Gt. Scotland Yd. SW1 —4B 82
Gt. Smith St. SW1 —2A 94
Gt. Suffolk St. SE1 —4C 84
Gt. Sutton St. EC1 —1C 72
Gt. Titchfield St. W1 —2C 68
Gt. Tower St. EC3 —1C 86
Gt. Windmill St. W1 —1F 81
Greek St. W1 —5A 70
Greencoat Pl. SW1 —4E 93
Greenfield St. E1 —3F 75
Green St. W1 —1F 79
Greenwell St. W1 —1C 68
Grenville Pl. SW7 —3D 89
Grenville St. WC1 —1C 70
Gresham St. EC2 —4E 73
Gresse St. W1 —3F 69
Greville St. EC1 —3A 72
Greycoat Pl. SW1 —3F 93
Greycoat St. SW1 —3F 93
Grosvenor Cres. SW1 —1A 92
Grosvenor Gdns. SW1 —2B 92
Grosvenor Ga. W1 —2F 79
Grosvenor Pl. SW1 —1A 92
Grosvenor Sq. W1 —1A 80
Grosvenor St. W1 —1B 80
Grove End Rd. NW8 —1A 58
  (in two parts)
Guilford St. WC1 —1C 70

Half Moon St. W1 —3C 80
Halkin St. SW1 —1A 92
Hamilton Pl. W1 —4A 80
Hampstead Rd. NW1 —2D 61
Hanbury St. E1 —2E 75

Mandeville Pl. W1 —4A 68
Manningtree St. E1 —4F 75
Mansell St. E1 —5E 75
Maple St. W1 —2D 69
Marchmont St. WC1 —5B 62
Margaret St. W1 —4C 68
Margery St. WC1 —4F 63
Markham St. SW3 —5C 90
Mark La. EC3 —1C 86
Marlborough Rd. SW1 —4E 81
Marloes Rd. W8 —3B 88
Marshall St. W1 —5E 69
Marshalsea Rd. SE1 —5E 85
Marsham St. SW1 —3A 94
Marylands Rd. W9 —1A 64
Marylebone Fly-Over. W1 —3F 65
Marylebone High St. W1 —2A 68
Marylebone La. W1 —3A 68
Marylebone Rd. NW1 —2C 66
Mecklenburgh Pl. WC1 —5D 63
Mecklenburgh Sq. WC1 —5D 63
Medburn St. NW1 —1F 61
Melcombe St. NW1 —1E 67
Melton St. NW1 —4E 61
Mews St. E1 —3F 87
Meymott St. SE1 —4B 84
Middlesex St. E1 —3C 74
Middle Temple La. EC4 —5F 71
Midland Rd. NW1 —2A 62
Millbank. SW1 —3B 94
Millman St. WC1 —1D 71
Mill St. SE1 —5E 87
Mill St. W1 —1C 80
Milner St. SW3 —4D 91
Milton St. EC2 —2F 73
Mincing La. EC3 —1B 86
Minories. EC3 —5D 75
Molyneux St. W1 —3C 66
Monck St. SW1 —3A 94
Monmouth St. WC2 —5B 70
Montague Pl. WC1 —2A 70
Montague St. EC1 —3D 73
Montague St. WC1 —2B 70
Montagu Pl. W1 —3D 67
Montagu Sq. W1 —3E 67
Montagu St. W1 —4E 67
Montpelier Sq. SW7 —1C 90
Montpelier St. SW7 —2C 90
Montpelier Wlk. SW7 —2C 90
Monument St. EC3 —1A 86
Moore St. SW3 —4D 91
Moorfields. EC2 —3F 73
Moorgate. EC2 —4F 73
Moor La. EC2 —3F 73
Moreton Pl. SW1 —5E 93
Moreton St. SW1 —5F 93
Moreton Ter. SW1 —5E 93
Morley St. SE1 —2A 96
Mornington Cres. NW1 —1D 61

Mornington Pl. NW1 —1C 60
Mornington St. NW1 —1C 60
Mornington Ter. NW1 —1C 60
Mortimer St. W1 —4D 69
Moscow Rd. W2 —2A 76
Mossop St. SW3 —4C 90
Motcomb St. SW1 —2F 91
Mt. Pleasant. WC1 —1F 71
Mount St. W1 —2F 79
Moxon St. W1 —3F 67
Muriel St. N1 —1E 63
Museum St. WC1 —3B 70
Myddelton Sq. EC1 —3F 63

Neal St. WC2 —5B 70
(in two parts)
Neathouse Pl. SW1 —4D 93
Nebraska St. SE1 —5F 85
Nevern Pl. SW5 —5A 88
Nevern Rd. SW5 —5A 88
Nevern Sq. SW5 —5A 88
Neville Ter. SW7 —5F 89
New Bond St. W1 —5B 68
New Bri. St. EC4 —5B 72
New Burlington St. W1 —1D 81
Newburn St. SE11 —5E 95
New Cavendish St. W1 —3A 68
New Change. EC4 —5D 73
Newcomen St. SE1 —5F 85
New Compton St. WC2 —5A 70
New Fetter La. EC4 —4A 72
Newgate St. EC1 —4C 72
Newington Butts. SE11 —5C 96
New Inn Yd. EC2 —1C 74
Newman St. W1 —3E 69
New North St. WC1 —2D 71
New Oxford St. WC1 —4A 70
Newport St. SE11 —4D 95
New Quebec St. W1 —5E 67
Newton St. WC2 —4C 70
New Wharf Rd. N1 —1C 62
Noble St. EC2 —4D 73
Noel St. W1 —5E 69
Norfolk Cres. W2 —4B 66
Norfolk Pl. W2 —4A 66
N. Audley St. W1 —5F 67
N. Carriage Dri. W2 —1B 78
Northdown St. N1 —1C 62
N. Gower St. NW1 —4E 61
Northington St. WC1 —1E 71
N. Ride. W2 —2A 78
Northumberland Av. WC2 —3B 82
North Wlk. W2 —2C 76
N. Wharf Rd. W2 —3F 65
Norton Folgate. E1 —2C 74
Notting Hill Ga. W11 —3A 76
Nottingham Pl. W1 —2F 67
Nottingham St. W1 —2F 67

Oakington Rd. W9 —1A 64
Oakley Sq. NW1 —1E 61
Observatory Gdns. W8 —5A 76
Old Bailey. EC4 —5C 72
Old Bond St. W1 —2D 81
Old Broad St. EC2 —4A 74
Old Brompton Rd. SW5 & SW7
—5D 89
Old Castle St. E1 —3D 75
Old Cavendish St. W1 —5C 68
Old Compton St. W1 —1F 81
Old Gloucester St. WC1 —2C 70
Old Marylebone Rd. NW1 —3C 66
Old Montague St. E1 —3F 75
Old Paradise St. SE11 —4D 95
Old Park La. W1 —4B 80
Old Pye St. SW1 —2F 93
Old Queen St. SW1 —1A 94
Old St. EC1 —1D 73
Onslow Gdns. SW7 —5F 89
Onslow Sq. SW7 —5A 90
Orange St. WC2 —2A 82
Orchard St. W1 —5F 67
Ordnance Hill. NW8 —1A 58
Ormonde Ter. NW8 —1D 59
Orsett Ter. W2 —4C 64
Osbert St. SW1 —5F 93
Osborn St. E1 —3E 75
Osnaburgh St. NW1 —5C 60
Osnaburgh Ter. NW1 —5C 60
Ossington St. W2 —2B 76
Ossulston St. NW1 —2A 62
Oswin St. SE11 —4C 96
Outer Circ. NW1 —3C 58
Ovington Gdns. SW3 —3C 90
Ovington Sq. SW3 —3C 90
Oxford Cir. W1 —5D 69
Oxford Sq. W2 —5B 66
Oxford St. W1 —5E 67

Paddington Basin. W2 —4F 65
Paddington Grn. W2 —2A 66
Paddington St. W1 —2F 67
Page St. SW1 —4F 93
Pakenham St. WC1 —4E 63
Palace Av. W8 —5C 76
Palace Gdns. M. W8 —3A 76
Palace Gdns. Ter. W8 —3A 76
Palace Ga. W8 —1D 89
Palace Grn. W8 —4B 76
Palace St. SW1 —2D 93
Pall Mall. SW1 —4E 81
Pall Mall E. SW1 —3A 82
Pancras Rd. NW1 —1F 61
Panton St. SW1 —2F 81
Park Cres. W1 —1B 68
Park La. W1 —1E 79
Park Pl. SW1 —3D 81
Park Pl. Vs. W2 —2E 65

Park Rd. NW8 & NW1 —4B 58
Park Sq. E. NW1 —5B 60
Park Sq. W. NW1 —1B 68
Park St. SE1 —3D 85
Park St. W1 —1F 79
Park Village E. NW1 —1B 60
Parkway. NW1 —1B 60
Parliament Sq. SW1 —1B 94
Parliament St. SW1 —5B 82
Paul St. EC2 —1A 74
Paternoster Sq. EC4 —7C 72
Paveley St. NW8 —4B 58
Pavilion Rd. SW1 —1E 91
Peel St. W8 —4A 76
Pelham Cres. SW7 —5B 90
Pelham Pl. SW7 —4B 90
Pelham St. SW7 —4A 90
Pembridge Gdns. W2 —2A 76
Pembridge Pl. W2 —1A 76
Pembridge Rd. W11 —2A 76
Pembridge Sq. W2 —1A 76
Pembridge Vs. W11 & W2 —1A 76
Pembroke Rd. W8 —4A 88
Pembroke Sq. W8 —3A 88
Pembroke Vs. W8 —4A 88
Penfold St. NW8 & NW1 —1A 66
Penton Pl. SE17 —5C 96
Penton Rise. WC1 —3E 63
Penton St. N1 —1F 63
Pentonville Rd. N1 —2D 63
Penywern Rd. SW5 —5B 88
Pepys St. EC3 —1C 86
Percy Cir. WC1 —3E 63
Percy St. W1 —3F 69
Petticoat La. E1 —3C 74
Petty France. SW1 —2E 93
Phillimore Gdns. W8 —1A 88
Phillimore Wlk. W8 —2A 88
Philpot La. EC3 —1B 86
Phoenix Pl. WC1 —5E 63
Phoenix Rd. NW1 —3F 61
Piccadilly. W1 —4C 80
Piccadilly Cir. W1 —2F 81
Pilgrim St. EC4 —5B 72
Pimlico Rd. SW1 —5F 91
Platt St. NW1 —1F 61
Plender St. NW1 —1D 61
Pocock St. SE1 —5C 84
Poland St. W1 —5E 69
Polygon Rd. NW1 —2F 61
Ponsonby Pl. SW1 —5A 94
Pont St. SW1 —3D 91
Porchester Gdns. W2 —1C 76
Porchester Pl. W2 —5C 66
Porchester Rd. W2 —4C 64
Porchester Sq. W2 —4C 64
Porchester Ter. W2 —1D 77
Porchester Ter. N. W2 —4C 64
Portland Pl. W1 —1B 68

INDEX TO EMBASSIES, LEGATIONS AND COMMONWEALTH REPRESENTATIVES

INDEX TO HOSPITALS

Find us on Facebook
facebook.com/azmaps

@AZmaps